IN THE N.
'NEW WORLD ORDER'

Manifestations of Decadent Powers
in World Politics

Amnon Reuveni

Mike Reiners
1/7/02

TEMPLE LODGE
London

Translated by Nicholas Nunhofer and Terry Boardman, and revised by Amnon Reuveni

Temple Lodge Publishing
51 Queen Caroline Street
London W6 9QL

Published by Temple Lodge 1996

Originally published in an earlier version in German under the title *In Namen der 'Neuen Weltordnung'* by Verlag am Goetheanum, Dornach, Switzerland, 1994

A catalogue record for this book is available from the British Library

ISBN 0 904693 81 3

Cover by S. Gulbekian. Map by Ib Ohlsson, *Foreign Affairs*
Typeset by Imprint Publicity Service, Crawley Down, Sussex
Printed and bound in Great Britain by Cromwell Press Limited, Broughton Gifford, Wiltshire

Contents

Introduction

Conventional attempts to look at the events of our time are still dominated by three prejudgements. First, it is usually taken for granted that present-day events are always caused by what has gone before. Secondly, it is assumed that politicians' decisions and strategies are largely opportunistic. Thirdly, it is therefore maintained that such strategies must be the result of short-term political plans.

The partly augmented articles in this book approach the problem from a radically different direction. Apart from Chapter 7, on 'Solidarity', which is published here for the first time, they were all written for the Swiss weekly magazine *Das Goetheanum* between 1993 and 1994, a period when the world was in a state of great upheaval. With the aid of Anthroposophy, they seek to contribute to a deeper understanding of the post-Cold War world situation. They proceed from the fundamental assumption that—first—the present is not *only* to be regarded as the outcome of the past. There are always upheavals in history that have a spiritual origin. Such spiritual impulses do, of course, work parallel to the external causes of events but, especially in times like the present, the spiritual impulses play a far stronger role. Secondly, that not only political opportunism should be considered but also *the spiritual forces working in the background* and the groups that attempt to exert an influence over politicians. This leads to the third presupposition of this work, namely, that such groups have a long-term strategy, which the politicians under their influence then try, more or less unconsciously, to carry out.

In many of his lectures, Rudolf Steiner speaks of spiritual

streams that exert an influence upon individual human beings, peoples, cultures, religions, and upon humanity as a whole.[1] It is always remarkable to observe just how relevant his observations, made over 70 years ago, are for the end of this century. Something of what he described in broad outlines has been taken up in this book and made concrete in application to various phenomena in the current world situation. All symptoms, however, merely point to the *spiritual origins* of the present world crisis. A certain knowledge of the basic written works of Rudolf Steiner and of the above-mentioned lectures on contemporary history are therefore essential for a true evaluation of the contents of this book.

*

The twentieth century will hold a special position in the collective memory of humanity for a long time to come. This is in part due to the fact that during this century there has, for the first time, arisen a *world civilization*. New concepts such as 'World War', 'global economy', 'World Bank' and 'world policeman' have been created to describe this new development and its consequences. These concepts, which attempt to define this sea change, all too often, however, show through their limitations the need for a *new form of thinking* that is capable of grasping this radically new world situation.

The old mentality, the old way of thinking, stems from quite different conditions when, for example, the earth was not yet covered with a vast, integrated communications network. One can often perceive how the old village mentality remains present in those watching television news reports in, say, Hamburg or Budapest, even when watching a report from the American news agency CNN that has been simultaneously transmitted and co-ordinated from Washington, London and South Africa. (It is not for nothing that CNN calls itself 'The World News Leader'.) The external development of technology to *global* and even *cosmic* dimensions and the conquering of space and time has been greeted by most people with astonishment, but without seeking a counterbalance through an inner expansion and 'conquering' of the life of the soul.

The origins of this world civilization can be traced back four hundred years to the 'discoveries', conquests and colonizations of previously unknown parts of the earth by the so-called West. The prerequisite for all this, however, was the emergence of the natural sciences and the industrial revolution. Because Britain has played a leading role in the race to conquer the earth since the beginning of the seventeenth century, the Anglo-Saxons have come to be strongly identified with the emergence of a world civilization, and their naked strivings for hegemony within this civilization have come in for much criticism. Over the course of time, however, this criticism has taken on a dangerous colouring. For behind the critical voices one can increasingly perceive opposition to the whole process of human development *itself*. In fact most of the criticism of western imperialism since the 1920s has lacked a differentiated, objective approach to this whole complex of problems, and instead has manifested as opposition towards the whole further development of a world civilization. Indeed, those who were truly able to hear what was going on could already over 70 years ago perceive that the impulse lurking behind this criticism is a desire to drive this new global civilization onto a path of steep decline.

*

This book will examine the geo-political plans and goals of various groups who are pursuing their own special interests based on their particular spiritual viewpoint. Their efforts, however, do actually knock human development out of balance, for the sources from which these groups obtain their inspiration are one-sided. Neither do they bring any healing forces for their own natural and cultural communities. They are powers that are attempting to lead world civilization as a whole away from a balanced course of development. *These powers then have a seductive nature.*

However, in the course of the twentieth century, mankind has been faced with a wholly new danger that cannot be merely described as seductive. This new force hides its true colours behind the mask of recognized methods of deviation and temptation. The driving impulse of this new force is purely the *will to destroy*. It has manifested most completely in the phenomenon of National Socialism. For the final aim of National Socialism was not just the final solution to the Jewish question *but also a final solution to the German question and thus the final solution to the European question.*

All over Europe at that time there were people who placed themselves at the service of these powers. For example, many of Himmler's SS troops were of non-German origin, and took part in 'the ultimate war' to end once and for all the European question through mass murder and wholesale destruction.[2] The same can be applied to the Nazi leadership in the last months of the Third Reich when the total destruction of Germany was ordered (in Hitler's 'Nero Command') with a battle 'down to the last man and the last cartridge' (Major General Hellmuth Reyman, commander of Berlin, on 12 March 1945). Alert observers were, however, able to see this immense potential for human and cultural destruction lying behind the seductive masks of the Nazis well before those serving these forces came into power in Germany in 1933. On 9 August 1932, Wilhelm Muelon (1878–1944), one of the most insightful Europeans of this century, wrote to Friederich Dessauer: 'In order to control the crazed mass of National Socialists, I would give my full support to the centrist politicians in Papen's Cabinet, for *National Socialists would wreak a trail of destruction through all humanity and human culture* [author's italics].'[3]

Those circles that support a world civilization but none-theless wish to direct it towards their own particular ends have their own concept of a new world order. This, however, is to be a quite particular form of world order. But for the successors of National Socialism (who today, in order to give themselves some credibility, often hypercritically refer to the National Socialist regime as 'criminal'), the development of a world civilization and all the accompanying plans for a new world order are simply a nightmare. For these powers of destruction do not wish to promote a new world order in any form whatsoever; rather they seek to lead the world to the quickest path of decline. If one reads today between the lines of much of the revisionist 'historical' literature (which is generally merely a straightforward revival of a Goebbels-type of propaganda rather than any real revision of history), behind the masks of the contemporary 'lovers of truth' and the 'middle-European patriots' who claim to be fighting so valiantly with the western imperialism of the new world order, one sees lurking the same lust for destruction that possessed the 'defenders of Germany' in the Nazi period. The fact that the chapter of this book which deals with this appears in the Appendix is in no way a reflection on its relative importance. This book concerns itself primarily with the powers of seduction, whose essential interest it is to direct the course of this new world civilization. It is for this reason that the chapter on the *powers of destruction* appears separately in the Appendix.

*

This Introduction has been written with the sombre feeling that humanity's present-day confusion is in many ways similar to that of the 30s. Particularly in Europe one must be wary that the very real dangers of seduction and destruction are not confused with one another. Confusing the two has already today nearly laid the European question to rest. A calm examination of the phenomenon of the new world order should therefore not obscure those other forces that are attempting to lead mankind into the abyss.

If one reads some of the literature available today on the theme of this book, one is in the main overwhelmed by the amount of information and the number of assertions made. This in itself can lead to the creation of a confused atmosphere into which all sorts of suggestions can be inserted. This book has been written with the opposite intention in mind. The author wishes to encourage the reader to check over each thought and each fact and so form an independent judgement on the contents. It is hoped that this book can be of use to all those who seek a better understanding of the times in which we live.

Amnon Reuveni
Dornach, 29 September 1994

1
'No One in this World is Irreplaceable'

A Look into the Background of
the American Political Tradition

With the end of the Russo-Japanese War, in the summer of
1905, the American railway magnate E.H. Harriman believed that the time had arrived to realize his global plans.
After gaining control over the railway lines between the
Atlantic and Pacific coasts, as well as the shipping lines
between America and Japan, he strove for an agreement
between Japan and Russia on the construction of a 'round-
the-world' railway and shipping system, for which his own
American network could serve as the model. In this way, by
means of the persuasive might of American monetary and
economic power, he hoped to export American culture deep
into Russia and Asia.

When he travelled with his whole family to Japan, E.H.
Harriman was received with full honours. Japanese politicians were more than prepared to do business with him. The
people, by contrast, were outraged by the start of the Ameri-
can-orchestrated peace talks with the Russians, and the
streets filled with anti-American demonstrations. Despite
these difficulties, Harriman was able to realize his intentions
and returned with a signed agreement in his pocket. But
while in San Francisco on his return journey he received a
telegram from the Japanese saying that they wished for
more time to consider the situation before going ahead. For
Harriman this meant that, to all intents and purposes, his
trip had failed.

The time was clearly not yet ripe for the realization of such plans. However, what lay behind this will for commercial domination of the world has now to a great extent already been achieved. Today the Anglo-Saxon world view is celebrating the triumph of its ideal of a market economy in almost all the countries of the ex-Communist bloc. The homeland of the American dream has, however, been faced with so much uncertainty and instability in the last third of this century (the humiliation in Vietnam and a long-term economic crisis) that many have feared for the continuance of its role as world leader.

Almost 80 years after E.H. Harriman's Asian journey, a decisive contribution towards the revival of the American dream was made by his son Averell Harriman (1891–1986) —who as a 14-year-old boy had accompanied his father on the trip to Japan—by means of the selection of a young president for the end of the century. He sought out someone who had undergone the 'right' preparation and possessed all the right qualities for the task. In Bill Clinton he found a candidate who, as a true Anglo-Saxon patriot[1] and graduate from three of the elite training schools for the American Establishment—Georgetown (the university for would-be diplomats), Oxford[2] and Yale—held all the necessary prerequisites for the position.

A few weeks after the early death of E.H. Harriman (on 9 September 1909) Rudolf Steiner spoke of his outlook, characterizing him as 'one of the few millionaires who have concerned themselves with thoughts of a universally human nature'. He then went on to quote E.H. Harriman's own maxim that 'No one in this world is irreplaceable and everyone can, after he has left this world, have his place taken up by someone else'.[3] Seven years later Steiner indicated that he had 'always wondered' how an American who 'could be counted as one of the leading figures of his time' could hold such a view.[4] In what follows we shall attempt a symptomatological study of the background to this viewpoint.

*

At the same time as E.H. Harriman died in October 1909, his eldest son Averell entered Yale University. The decision to go to this university was not in the first place determined by choice of subject matter; then as now it had far more to do with a future decision to join particular elite circles of the American establishment. Yale distinguishes itself from most American universities in that membership of some of its most important student brotherhoods (such as the Skull and Bones and the Scroll and Key) only shows its true significance after graduation. As a rule the remaining student societies, the *junior societies*, simply belong to the general milieu of the student period. One can only become a member of the *senior societies* of Yale and Harvard in one's final year and will thereafter be a member for life. For Averell Harriman, as the son of the great E.H., and therefore marked out to become 'someone and somebody', only the elite universities of Harvard and Yale could be considered. He had then, as he later explained, plumped for Yale and, in particular, for Skull and Bones.[5] (The 'best' of those who failed to get into Skull and Bones are allowed into Scroll and Key.)

As had been the tradition since the founding of Skull and Bones in 1833 the candidates for membership gathered together with their parents and friends, as well as some inquisitive onlookers, on 16 May 1912. They waited patiently in the pouring rain until exactly five o'clock when the election process began for the 15 who were to be initiated into the secrets of the brotherhood during the following night.[6] Even for Averell Harriman, who was the first to be chosen, membership of Skull and Bones opened up countless new possibilities. For, in contrast to his father who had had to expend a great deal of energy cultivating friendships with the right people, he now had, in addition to his millionaire's inheritance, won hundreds of brothers, many of whom held high positions in the government (such as W.H. Taft, then the president of the USA), on Wall Street, in the Press and almost all branches of life.

In 1920, together with his younger brother Roland, Averell Harriman founded an investment society that also opened branches in war-torn Europe. The two sons of E.H. were from earliest childhood raised in accordance with the strictest pedagogical traditions of the Anglo-Saxon aristocracy. The avowed aim of such an upbringing was to develop the mental and physical capacities that would enable young men to make their mark on the world. Such qualities, together with the enormous capital reserves that the brothers possessed, were to be of great assistance in carving out for themselves one of the mightiest positions in world finance. Their partner Prescott Bush (father of the later president George Bush), who entered the successful Wall Street firm of the two brothers in 1926, studied with Roland in Yale and was initiated into Skull and Bones with him in 1916. Over the course of the next 50 years he was to become one of the Harrimans' closest friends and co-workers. The fact that he, like his son, was a Republican never upset the Democrat Averell Harriman. Bush was an important participant in their key breakthrough in 1930 when the two Wall Street giants 'Harriman Brothers & Company' and 'Brown Brothers & Company' merged. Eight out of the twelve partners of the new firm were 'Bones-men'.

The new business of Brown Brothers Harriman & Company was soon a thriving concern and, despite the severity of the Great Depression—the worst this century—opened branches in many countries and became the largest private bank in North America. Nevertheless this success in business was not enough for Averell Harriman; he desired access to the political stage in order 'to be able to serve America even better'.

Harriman was an internationalist; he was one of those who foresaw the transference of world power from England to America and who personally promoted it. During the

Winston Churchill, Averell Harriman and Joseph Stalin at the
Kremlin, Moscow, August 1943.

Second World War he shuttled between London, Moscow
and Washington, first as a special envoy of President
Roosevelt and then later as the American ambassador to
Moscow. In 1942 and 1944 he travelled with Churchill to
Moscow in order to represent American interests during
negotiations with Stalin, in which the superpowers' future
spheres of influence in Europe were discussed.

During the war Harriman regularly carried secret documents between Moscow and London. The code number of
the briefcase in which he carried them was 322.[7] This is the
'sacred number' of Skull and Bones, which traces its tradition and ritual date back to ancient Greece. According to this
tradition it was the orator Demosthenes, who committed
suicide in 322 BC,[8] who founded the brotherhood. Over the
door of the windowless, Egyptian-style 'temple' of the Skull
and Bones society stands the number 322. Even during the

war Averell Harriman always strove to attend the society reunions that were held every year in the building on Long Island. Many know that Skull and Bones exists. Yet the rituals and content of meetings have been guarded with the utmost secrecy by their members. Harriman freely spoke in such gatherings about state secrets with complete trust in his fellow 'brothers of the number 322'.

Harriman remained active as a special emissary throughout the Cold War. He was continuously sent to the Kremlin by Truman, Kennedy, Johnson and even Nixon and Carter (his last visit was to Andropov in 1983 at the age of 91). He cultivated friendly relations with both Stalin and Krushchev. Aside from this he took care to see that the Marshall Plan, which he supervised in the years 1948–50, was rapidly implemented. He served as secretary of commerce, as governor of New York, and held a whole series of prominent positions at the Foreign Ministry. One of the greatest architects of the post-war world order, even in old age his toughness enabled him to exert more influence than many younger politicians.

Nonetheless, anyone who studies this extraordinary biography must concede that it was not the forces of inner initiative of the individuality of Harriman that played the central role in all the significant occurrences of his rich life. It was much more the forces of the non-individualized consciousness soul, developed through training to a very high degree, that worked through him. He was the perfect pupil and servant of a particular system and his ideals and motivation had their origin almost exclusively in that system. With total loyalty and dedication he worked right up until his death (on 26 July 1986) for the spreading of the 'American way of life' and for the position of the United States as *the* superpower of the coming era. He thus served many of the Republican and all of the Democratic presidents this century (with the exception of Woodrow Wilson and Clinton).

Harriman II's Search for a President for the New Generation

At the beginning of the 1980s Harriman and his wife Pamela Churchill-Harriman[9] began to look for a Democratic alternative for the post-Reagan and Bush era. Since Harriman had already had 70 years' experience playing according to Washington's rules, he knew full well that after Bush (the son of his colleague and himself a trusted 'Bones brother') a Democrat would move into the White House. He now used all his talents and connections for his last great project: the choosing of an appropriate candidate for president at the end of this century. In their majestic salon, which became Washington's unofficial centre of power in the 80s, his wife Pamela organized discussion evenings for prominent people from Wall Street, the Democratic party and various other walks of life. In meeting Bill Clinton and Al Gore, the 90-year-old Harriman was looking for what he called 'young blood'. As his widow explained in an interview immediately following Clinton's election victory: 'He was the one who sought them out . . . invited them to our home, talked to them about past presidencies and the crises their generation faces.'[10] Following that, Clinton was the first person whom Pamela Harriman chose to serve on the board of 'Democrats for the 80s', a political group which originated in their discussion evenings.

'Democrats for the 80s' was, however, only the preparatory stage. In 1985 some of the politicians from the Harrimans' circle founded the 'Democratic Leadership Council' (DLC). At that time Clinton, who became the first speaker of the DLC, was the governor of Arkansas. The euphoria of the Reagan years was reaching its zenith. The members of the DLC took it upon themselves to take the Democratic party out of the unpopular left-liberal corner it was then in. They were, however, soon attacked by the

Averell Harriman with John F. Kennedy outside the White
House (1961).

majority of the Democrats for being too conservative and Republican in their leanings (not least due to the friendly relations which the Harrimans traditionally cultivated with Republicans such as Bush and Baker).

Nevertheless, the DLC was in possession of the best prerequisites of political success: money and connections. Even after the death of her husband Averell in 1986 Pamela Harriman remained *the* salon lady of Washington and regularly invited rich friends to evening receptions in which DLC supporters could meet and give generously ('never less than $10,000'). With all the millions she collected in this way the DLC was able to employ the best electioneering strategists and to finance a candidate for the Democratic contest. In 1990 Clinton was elected as president of the DLC, and then, with this power structure behind him, went on to win the Democratic nomination at the beginning of 1992 and then the presidential election itself. After his victory, Pamela Harriman received so many messages of congratulation that it was as if she herself had won the election. At the end of March 1993 Clinton appointed her American ambassador to France.

It could of course be maintained that Harriman was only considering the best interests of the Democratic Party when he sought out Clinton. For Harriman, though, the American party rivalries were an illusion. During occasional conversations with friends on foreign policy issues he had to be frequently reminded of his Democratic allegiances. In short: Harriman concerned himself with the broader questions of American politics. He knew that, considered from a higher vantage point, the dualistic system of politics in America merely serves to distract the will and the consciousness of the voters. While the political parties fight, the most important questions of policy in the USA (and not only there) are agreed upon behind closed doors, where questions of party affiliation are of no account whatsoever. Rudolf Steiner once said: 'However grotesque it might at first seem, one can say that Hegel's philosophy is in a certain way the benchmark of the secret teachings of the West.'[11] Although Steiner refers to other areas of Hegel's philosophy in this lecture, it is interesting to note that Hegel's philosophy, based as it is on the superiority of synthesis over thesis and antithesis, actually became a way of life for people such as Harriman. In brotherhoods such as Skull and Bones the members of the opposing parties know only too well that the attaining of *synthesis* can only profit from the opposition between thesis and antithesis. They therefore seek actively to promote such contradictions, both in domestic politics and foreign affairs. This is not to say that they artificially engender conflicts, merely that they foster the latent potential for conflict. Anyway, they have one strict rule: one must keep the contradictions and conflicts under control. Otherwise no one, not even the cleverest Skull and Bones member, can profit from it.[12]

*

When Rudolf Steiner, in the above-mentioned lecture,[13] says about Harriman's belief that no one is irreplaceable, 'that such an Americanism can only come out of the most profound lack of knowledge of real life', he is in no way decrying America. For in the same lecture he speaks with gratitude about the attempts of a friend who before he died had held a high post in Freemasonry (the dominant spiritual stream of the West) to imbue this stream 'with spiritual science'. It is interesting to note how Steiner immediately afterwards speaks of Harriman's belief.

What stands after all behind the assertion that 'no one is irreplaceable in this world'? Is this not an expression of the deep connection between E.H. Harriman and a cultural stream in which the individual and his or her fate are subordinated to 'the great missions and ideals' of a people? 'The truth,' continues Steiner, 'is actually the exact opposite

. . . no one can be replaced in relation to everything he was in life.' Steiner's view, as he goes on to elaborate, is one that above all builds upon the karma or destiny of the individual human life. In other words: the spiritual stream that is represented by Rudolf Steiner wishes to create a culture the life and power of which stems from the individual. The brotherhoods-culture of the West, which trains the instinctive and thus vigorous power of the consciousness soul, demands a total willingness to sacrifice oneself in favour of the system. If this were balanced with an emphasis on the importance of the 'I am' and the significance of karma then it could play a significantly more constructive role. On the other hand, what has for a long time been practised in the West, namely, the overlooking of the development of the free human spirit, the avoidance of the question of individual karma and the focusing solely upon the elemental forces of the consciousness soul, the natural gift of the Anglo-Saxon people, is becoming increasingly dangerous. For the political (and not only the political) culture of the United States, which still receives its impulses from the brotherhoods, is presently sinking rapidly into ever greater decadence, irrespective of Bill Clinton's youth.

2
The Legacy of Cecil Rhodes

From the British Empire to *Pax Americana*

'To Rhodes the British Empire was to be one of the revelations of human history, a new heaven and a new earth.'
James Morris, *Pax Britannica*

Many Oxford colleges have long supplemented their income by letting out some of their rooms to conference participants over the summer vacation period. The organizers of the 1922 public conference entitled 'Spiritual Values in Education and Social Life' particularly valued Manchester College, which with its joint accommodation for both professors and students was modelled on the style of the very first Oxford colleges. Rudolf Steiner's lectures at Oxford were therefore held in a kind of medieval, monastic atmosphere. Among his listeners were many students, some professors and anthroposophical friends. The gathering was initiated by English anthroposophists who were both convinced of the necessity to reform social life and also wished to make the model of Waldorf education better known in Great Britain.[1]

In order to gain as wide an echo in the public domain as possible, the organizers of the conference sought the patronage of many prominent figures in political and economic circles of the time. Among others, they received the support of the British education minister, Professor H.A.L. Fisher, under whose patronage the conference was then held.

Professor H.A.L. Fisher is also well known as an historian;

his book *History of Europe* (1936) has become a classic in its field. The fact that it was he who took upon himself the overall patronage of this anthroposophical conference is in itself an interesting historical symptom. For it was just here, in Oxford, that Rudolf Steiner spoke most persistently of the urgent need to transform the forces and structures from the past—which one can still to this day very strongly experience at Oxford—into impulses that are appropriate for the modern age. And yet H.A.L. Fisher was himself one of the most important representatives in Great Britain of that stream which guards the 'noble traditions'[2] of the past, and whose aim it is to preserve the spirit of the Middle Ages right up into the present day. In the years between 1925 and 1940 Fisher was one of the trustees of the Rhodes Trust. This trust supervised the endowments made by Cecil Rhodes[3] in his last will for the famous Rhodes Scholarship awards.

*

Fisher's path to this post led via Oxford. As a young man he began his studies in 1883 at New College. Here he got to know Alfred Milner, later War Minister, who was then a Fellow of the college. It was a typical Oxford meeting, both remaining closely connected with one another until Milner's death in 1925. After Fisher had taken his finals Milner suggested he stay on at Oxford as a lecturer and Fellow of the college. They worked together at New College until 1897. Then Cecil Rhodes named Milner, his old Oxford University pal, to be his successor as governor of the Cape Colony in South Africa.

However, old friends who are not just Fellows of the same college but also belong to the same Masonic brotherhood (as is sometimes even today still the case in Oxford) very often stay in close touch with each other. When Lloyd George formed his ultimate war Cabinet at the end of 1916 he called, among others, upon Milner who then went on to play a very decisive role in the First World War, first as minister without portfolio and then as war minister. But Milner had not forgotten his friend Fisher, who was then called, on his recommendation, to the Cabinet. After the war Milner was able, as colonial secretary, to further his stridently imperialistic aims without arousing too much opposition. Until 1922 he worked closely with Fisher on this task. Their common aim was the construction and consolidation of an Anglo-Saxon world culture, in accordance with the plans of Cecil Rhodes. It was in this spirit that Milner worked as one of those most engaged in carrying out the testament of Cecil Rhodes.

In the autumn of 1891 Rhodes wrote in an open letter to his friend the occultist W.T. Stead, one of the most influential journalists in England at that time:

> It would have been better for Europe if he [Napoleon] had carried out his idea of universal monarchy; he might have succeeded if he had hit on the idea of granting self-government to the component parts. Still, I will own tradition, race and diverse languages acted against his dream; all these do not exist as to the present English-speaking world, and apart from this union is the sacred duty of taking the responsibility of the still uncivilized parts of the world ... What a scope and what a horizon of work at any rate, for the next two centuries, the best energies of the best people in the world; perfectly feasible, but needing an organization, for it is impossible for one human atom to complete anything, much less such an idea as this requiring the devotion of the best souls of the next 200 years. There are three essentials: 1) the plan duly weighed and agreed to; 2) the first organization; 3) the seizure of the wealth necessary.[4]

*

When Rhodes went to Oxford in the summer of 1873 he was

initially rejected by University College, the self-same college
to which, roughly one hundred years later, Bill Clinton
attended through his Rhodes Scholarship. Following this
rebuff, Rhodes began his studies at Oriel College instead.
There he first attended lectures by John Ruskin, Professor of
Art History, whose ideas had been causing something of a
sensation among the Oxford student population for the
previous three years. Ruskin argued that the most worthy of
all traditions, that of the British aristocracy, would slip into
an inexorable decline unless it could find ways of rejuvenat-
ing itself. The sole possibility for this, according to Ruskin,
lay in the active extension and promulgation of its traditions
of loyalty, respectability, law and order, self-discipline, etc.
to the global level.[5] For Rhodes, these words were a source
of inspiration; he carried the manuscript with him for nearly
30 years. In his various wills (all in all he wrote seven
appendages to his will) he himself spoke in a very similar
way of the world mission of British civilization. To achieve
his aims he wished to found a secret society which, in its
organizational structure, was to be a 'copy of the Order of
the Jesuits'.[6]

*

Rudolf Steiner spoke on a great number of occasions about
particular western brotherhoods, whose conception of
their mission within the fifth post-Atlantean epoch can be
summarized as follows: 'There must arise something in
the West—out of those people that actually form the fifth
sub-race—that is a kind of copy of the papacy.'[7] For it is
the viewpoint of these lodges that, following centuries in
which Rome has been the educator of European humanity,
it is now the task of British civilization to put its stamp
upon the whole world. The fact that Cecil Rhodes was
himself whole-heartedly of this opinion is attested to by
many of his utterances. As, for example, in his third testa-

ment in 1888 when he states that the civilizing mission of the British Empire would be furthered by the founding of a secret society 'which will, as far as is possible, be constructed in the manner of the Jesuit Order'. The words 'Roman Catholic religion' have thus simply been replaced by the designation 'British Empire'.[8]

Already in 1877 the young Rhodes regarded himself as the new Loyola,[9] the founder of a secret, world-embracing organization for the aims of which 'many thousands of people' would readily dedicate themselves.[10] At that time, he had neither the financial nor social resources necessary for such an undertaking. Fourteen years later, however, he was one of the richest people in the world, with an annual income of over one million pounds. As prime minister of the Cape Colony and the holder of a seat in the British Parliament, he was also one of the most influential people in the Empire.

The contemporary American professor of history, Carroll Quigley,[11] describes the origins and emergence of this Order in the Rhodesian mould. He gives a detailed insider account of Rhodes's Order in his book *The Anglo-American Establishment* and a much more general view of this story in his later book *Tragedy and Hope*. While he fails to give his sources in *Tragedy and Hope*—a remarkable omission for a scientific book of this nature—*The Anglo-American Establishment* has a detailed reference index. If one studies these two books together, one comes to a remarkably comprehensive delving into the background events to the western political scene in this century, something that Rudolf Steiner had already gone into the occult meaning of in the years 1915–23.

*

According to Quigley's description, the long planned-for secret society was founded among a close circle of friends on 5 February 1891. Its founding members were Cecil

Rhodes, William T. Stead and Lord Esher (friend and advisor to Queen Victoria). Soon some other well-known personalities, such as the Earl of Rosebery, Arthur James Balfour, Nathan Rothschild, Alfred Milner and H.A.L. Fisher, were also initiated into the society which at first bore the name of 'The Secret Society of Cecil Rhodes'. The aim of the society was not simply the founding of another cultic brotherhood, for most of the members were in any case already Freemasons. The aim of this group of people, who all shared a common cultural and spiritual background in being Oxbridge graduates, was the founding of a 'Holy Empire' just as Ruskin had envisaged. The task called for clandestine activity and support, for the realizing of the group's aims could not be undertaken in the glare of publicity.

For Rhodes and his comrades the democratic system constituted a significant problem. For in order to realize long-term aims such as theirs requires stable political and ideological relations, but in a democracy one can never be certain which direction a new government might take. They therefore considered it the most important task of their secret society to create new organizations and institutions that would run parallel to the political system and would promote the ideals of an Anglo-Saxon world leadership. Such institutions would above all conduct their own independent scientific research into political issues and continuously lend support to the group without being influenced by the swings of the political pendulum. The ruling democratic system should learn to respect the thinking of such institutions and would—unofficially of course—follow their general guidance. In line with such intentions, libraries, stipendiums and university chairs were funded (among which special attention was paid to non-state universities such as Oxford, Harvard and Yale). Through these and other 'propaganda channels' the ideals of the 'Anglo-Saxon sympathizers' were to be spread.

Cecil Rhodes.

Lord Alfred Milner.

Up until the death of Rhodes the group concerned itself chiefly with gathering the necessary financial means for its work and enlisting the sympathy of influential people who, unlike committed members of the group, often did not know of the existence of the secret society. Rhodes had determined that never more than three people should lead the group. He possessed an uncanny understanding for the power of money and was convinced that huge financial sums would be needed to realize his aims. His weak health meant that he often felt the nearness of death, hence the numerous wills and testaments in which he expressed his ideals. His central aim was always the consolidation of an Anglo-Saxon world empire, for the accomplishment of which he even did not exclude the possibility of a reunion of Great Britain with the United States. He had no difficulty imagining Washington as the capital city of this empire! Most of his plans, however, were only realized after his death. It was his follower Alfred Milner who then, in a somewhat modified form, put them into practice.

When Milner took up his post in South Africa he gathered around him a group of young people who later followed him back to England. These young idealists, who were called 'Milner's Kindergarten', were quite willing to go through fire in order to realize the holy aim of civilizing the world's population in accordance with the great British example. They worked on two levels: officially they took up important political positions—Philip Kerr, for example, became the private secretary to Lloyd George—while unofficially they formed an association called 'The Round Table'.

Between 1905 and 1910 branches of this Round Table group were formed throughout the Empire. In the periodical *The Round Table*, H.V. Hodson characterized many years later the founders of this group as follows: 'Their backgrounds were alike; all had been at public schools and Oxford; four of them were fellows of All Souls. They were capable, hardworking and idealistic. They were imperial idealists, having deep faith in the value of the British Empire to all mankind, besides its own peoples, and in the civilizing mission of Britain and her daughter nations.'[12]

Here we can meet a symptom of some remnants of the old missionary efforts in the Anglo-Saxon West. From the most ancient times up until the Middle Ages there existed the order of the initiate Arthur. His knights, the Knights of the Round Table, had the task to civilize European culture.

> Such was the Round Table: King Arthur at the centre, surrounded by the twelve, above each of whom a zodiacal symbol was displayed, indicating the particular cosmic influence with which he was associated. Civilizing forces went out from this place to Europe. It was here that King Arthur and his twelve knights drew into themselves from the sun the strength wherewith to set forth on their mighty expeditions through Europe in order to battle with the wild, demonic powers of old, still dominating large masses of the population, and drive them out of people. Under the guidance and direction of King Arthur, *these twelve were battling for outer civilization* [author's italics].[13]

It is difficult to say to what extent the knights of Milner's Round Table knew of this occult background. But a man like W.T. Stead, who was very close to Rhodes and Milner, and, as both spiritualist and a colleague, was well acquainted with Annie Besant, would certainly have been aware of these connections.

From Washington to the Spiritual Home of the Anglo-Saxon World

When the 18-year-old Bill Clinton arrived at the School of Foreign Service at Jesuit-run Georgetown University in 1964, the man who he later called 'my great teacher', Carroll

Quigley, was working on his book *Tragedy and Hope, A History of the World in Our Time.* Quigley had already written two books. The manuscript of the first, *The Anglo-American Establishment,* had been ready for publication in 1949. But at that time he could not find a publisher willing to publish it, for this book was the result of an intensive study of the secret society around Rhodes and Milner. It must be that those circles could not allow his research, the product of an Oxford insider,[14] to reveal their activities to the world. So the manuscript sank out of sight for a long time. He could hardly wonder at this fate, however, for he himself had described how these groups exert an especially strong hold on the media and publishing houses! The book was first published in 1981, four years after his death.

In most of the Rhodes biographies it is said that his seventh and last testament overrides the previous ones in which he talks of the founding of a secret society. Quigley, however, maintains that the seventh testament is rather the last stage in a development process and that in the Rhodes Scholarship the founder of the secret society created the instrument for attaining his old goals.

During his studies in Washington Bill Clinton wrote to a friend that the professors wished him to apply for a Rhodes Scholarship but that he did not think he stood the slightest chance of getting one.[15] One of the professors who had urged him to go for 'one of the most prestigious scholarships in the United States' was Carroll Quigley. Harold Snider, a university friend of Clinton's, wrote: 'The toughest freshman course in the School of Foreign Service was Development of Civilization, taught by Professor Carroll Quigley ... Bill and I found him fascinating, electrifying and brilliant. He inspired in both of us a sense of personal responsibility and an eagerness to enter public service. Dr Quigley encouraged us both to go to England to do graduate work. I know that he wrote letters of recommendation for both of us and that he was very proud and pleased that we both went on to study at Oxford. Dr Quigley was our mentor and friend. He left an indelible impression on our lives.'[16]

All this took place in the years 1966/7. It was at just that time that Quigley's monumental work *Tragedy and Hope* appeared from the well-known Macmillan publishing house. In the 1,300 pages of this book Quigley revealed further results of his research into the Rhodes-Milner group, but in a considerably more compromised form than in his earlier work *The Anglo-American Establishment*. It is not unreasonable to suppose that his elite student Clinton would have read this work and therefore would have known that the Rhodes Scholarship was one of the most important means by which these secret societies realized their aims.

Nevertheless, apart from Clinton there were other people reading this book. Even the watered down analysis in *Tragedy and Hope* contained enough information to awaken the interest of American conspiracy theorists, especially as this time Quigley revealed also the American section of this secret society. One of these, a former FBI officer W.C. Skousen, asked for Quigley's permission to quote from this book in a small publication of his own. Despite Quigley's refusal he nonetheless went ahead and published his small book *The Naked Capitalist* in which he dealt in detail with the most controversial aspects of Quigley's book. This then gave the opportunity for a whole number of authors to discuss Quigley's revelations in a series of articles.

After this, *Tragedy and Hope* suddenly disappeared from the bookshops. Macmillan said that the book was out of print and that no further editions were being planned. What was even stranger was that some of the copies had also disappeared from state and university libraries. By the beginning of 1968, 16 months after its first appearance, this book had become a rarity, with single copies changing hands at anything between $250 and $400. Only in 1974 was a second edition brought out by another publishing house. At the end of 1975 Quigley wrote in a letter how his book had

Professor Carroll Quigley (1910-1977).

been deliberately suppressed: 'My publisher stopped sell-
ing it in 1968 and told me that he would reprint (but in 1974
he told my lawyer that the plates had been destroyed in
1968)!' In other words Macmillan had consistently stalled on
the matter until finally, he realized, 'they lied to me but
prevented me from regaining publication rights'.[17]

In 1968, just as the debate on the book *Tragedy and Hope*
reached its zenith, Quigley's pupil Clinton went to Oxford
as a Rhodes Scholar. For Quigley, who himself did not
regard the aims of the Rhodes-Milner group at all negatively, but who had merely broken the code of secrecy,
Oxford, with its 'headquarters', Rhodes House, was his
spiritual home. For he himself said that he regarded himself
as a true representative of the Anglo-Saxon tradition. The
one thing that separated him from the Rhodes-Milner
group was his conviction that such an historically significant organization should be publicly known about. It was
against this background then that he sent his best pupil to
Oxford, to the 'spiritual homeland of the Anglo-Saxons'.

In order to enter Rhodes House as a Rhodes Scholar
Clinton had to fulfil some difficult requirements. From the
85 Rhodes Scholarships that are awarded each year, 32 go to
the United States, 18 to former countries of the British
Empire and three to Germany (which was Rhodes's way of
honouring the family connection between the British throne
and the House of the Hohenzollerns). The candidate must be
between 20 and 26 years of age and be single. But above all
he must possess the right character traits as laid down by
Cecil Rhodes. Women have been able to apply since 1977,
but this is only as a result of British legislation on sexual
equality which was launched because of the tradition of the
Rhodes Trust. Unofficial support can be of considerable aid
in getting the Scholarship. Clinton, for example, owed his
success mainly to the recommendation of the well-known
Rhodes Scholar Senator Fulbright.[18]

Since 1902 the Rhodes Trust has been administered by

The 'Rhodes Scholar' Bill Clinton receives an honorary doctorate from Oxford University on 8 June 1994.

seven trustees as stipulated by Rhodes himself. Up until his death in 1925 Milner took care to ensure that additional millions were put into the Trust to guarantee its financial future. (In 1991 the Trust's assets were officially valued at £107,225,000.) Fisher was named as a trustee in 1925.

Rhodes House (which was opened in 1928, even though building work had only begun three years earlier)[19] became the centre of all initiatives arising out of the spirit of Cecil Rhodes. Institutions such as the Royal Institute of International Affairs and its American affiliate, the Council on Foreign Relations, have ever since been controlled almost exclusively by Oxbridge graduates. The tasks of these institutes go well beyond the mere proffering of advice. For the last 70 years or so they have been the main determiners of British and American foreign policy.

*

Ninety years after the death of Cecil Rhodes, the Rhodes Scholar Clinton was elected president of the United States. Understandably, some of his friends from Oxford and Yale moved with him to the White House.[20] Since 1902, however, the world has fundamentally changed: two world wars, atomic weaponry and computer technology are only some aspects of the far-reaching changes that have taken place. The origins of these changes are to be found in particular spiritual impulses and counter-impulses. Already in the 20s the group around Milner had given up Rhodes's idea of a US-British Confederation and had started looking for an alternative. This eventually took on the form of a community of ex-colonies, founded in 1931 as the 'British Commonwealth of Nations'. Today the 50-member nations of the Commonwealth only very loosely co-ordinate their political and economic aims, but the Queen is still a kind of head of state for them and in most of the countries of the Commonwealth the education system as well as the government and the legal system are all very strongly based upon the structures bequeathed them by the British Empire. One needs to think no further than the role which the English language plays in the world today—almost 80 per cent of scientific articles are published in English, and something between 1.2 and 1.6 billion people speak more or less fluent English as their first foreign language[21]—and the significance and power of the role played by the president of the United States to ask oneself how far the ideals of Cecil Rhodes have remained a Utopian dream or actually become a reality.

3
'The West Versus the Rest'

The Search for a Replacement to the Cold War

By the summer of 1993, the great debate that had flared up two years before in America over the economic recession had more or less fallen completely silent. The figures showed a modest but stable recovery; the sort of structural problems that were plaguing a reunited Germany at that time, for example, only played a minor part. The American public once again found time to consider foreign policy, and American foreign policy in Somalia and Haiti came in for some heavy criticism. The neo-isolationists (who spoke for many) maintained that the United States should only intervene abroad militarily in cases of self-defence. Against this, many hawkish experts such as Henry Kissinger called for a new and clearly defined course for the foreign policy of 'the world's only remaining superpower'. But where should the guiding thoughts for such policies come from? For the new era did not even have its own name. It was simply termed the 'epoch after the change' or the 'post-Cold War era'.

'The Clinton administration,' said the national security advisor Anthony Lake, 'is the first since the Truman era that in foreign policy has not had a single defining issue against which it could define itself.' It had not always been easy, he went on, for earlier administrations to answer the central question: 'What form will containment of the Soviet Union and Communism take?' But at least the question was already given. The Clinton administration, he said, 'is being asked both to define the questions and to provide the answers'.[1]

For more than 40 years the populations of the western hemisphere had lived with the picture of the Red terror. Yet today many experts are admitting that this danger was greatly exaggerated. For example, until very recently the Soviet production of enriched uranium was estimated to be double the amount it actually was. This false estimate was partly responsible for the fact that the absurd production of these extremely dangerous materials was continued in the United States until 1990. The same thing applied to the Red Army and its allies: their strengths and numbers were also systematically overestimated. Behind the outer conflict, however, the relationship between the Soviet Union and the United States was often not at all bad. This has been demonstrated, for example, by Professor Anthony Sutton in his three-volume work *Western Technology and Soviet Economic Development 1917–1965* in which, based on State Department data and documents, he demonstrates that the American Government continuously lent its arch-enemy technological and financial aid. Politicians such as Averell Harrimann and Nikita Krushchev were not the only ones who cultivated a good relationship across the Iron Curtain.

Rudolf Steiner once said that there is a 'huge discrepancy'[2] between the values and judgements publicly stated in the English-speaking world and the deeds of the West in international affairs. Public attitudes are imbued with strongly idealistic motives, the origins and influences of which are to be found on more or less unconscious levels. An example of this kind of working with ideals is in the following words of Margaret Thatcher: 'We are a free country and that is why we will campaign world-wide against every country that does not uphold freedom and fairness . . . That is why we fought the Falklands War and is also why we freed Kuwait from Saddam Hussein' (*Der Spiegel*, 25 October 1993). Freedom, democracy, pluralism and human rights—these are the great ideals of the West. They are indeed manifest in a notable number of laws and organizations that show a genuine striving to realize these ideals, for in them lies the true historical task of the West! But it is in the very circles that hold a key influence over politicians and the public that other interests work.

*

In the most important American foreign policy periodical *Foreign Affairs* there appeared, in the summer edition of 1993, a leading article by the Harvard University professor Samuel P. Huntington entitled 'The Clash of Civilizations?' Perceptive readers could not miss an important symptom here, namely, the contradiction between the question mark in the title and the absolute certainty with which Huntington prophesies that the era of the Cold War will be followed by an era in which conflicts will take place between different civilizations and cultures! In the 28 pages of his article Huntington gives a comprehensive overview of the present political situation. The systematic and lively way in which he characterizes all the large as well as all the small cultures, states and religions and analyses their interrelationships is both breathtaking and rather astonishing. With an extraordinary degree of conviction he comes to the conclusion that the ideological conflict between Communism and western liberalism that ruled during the Cold War era will be replaced by a new period marked by the clash of civilizations.[3] Against this background, a conflict between western civilization and the rest of the world is seen as the most inevitable scenario: 'A West at the peak of its power confronts non-Wests that increasingly have the desire, the will and the resources to shape the world in non-western ways,' writes Huntington (p. 26).

The Gulf War is, for Huntington, the first example of this new 'inter-civilizational' form of conflict. For the Gulf War was actually a war between the West and 'Islamic civilization'. Other examples of such a new type of conflict can be found in Bosnia, where 'Bosnian Muslims', 'Orthodox Serbs' and 'western Croats' were all fighting one another, and in the Caucasus where Muslims and eastern Christians are locked in conflict. The greatest danger for western hegemony is, according to Huntington, a drawing together of the Islamic with the Confucian 'civilization' (China, Taiwan, Singapore and Hong Kong). With regard to Russia's future Huntington also has a gloomy prophecy. Russia, he says, essentially belongs not to western civilization but to *Euro-Asian* civilization. 'If as the Russians stop behaving like Marxists they reject liberal democracy and begin behaving like Russians but not like westerners, the relations between Russia and the West could again become distant and conflictual' (p. 45). And even more clearly formulated: 'The Velvet Curtain of culture has replaced the Iron Curtain of ideology as the most significant dividing line in Europe. As the events in Yugoslavia show, it is not only a line of difference; it is also at times a line of *bloody* conflict [author's italics]' (p. 31).

This article gives one the impression that it is either the result of an individual intuition or the fruit of intensive group work. However, it is highly probable that it was the result of both, for it is most certainly also the result of a group inspiration within the American establishment. In order to elaborate on this assertion, it is necessary to recall that Huntington's article appeared at a time when discussion on the future role of the West and the institutions that it controls (such as NATO and the UN, according to Huntington) was at its height in the US. Although the article appeared to draw considerable criticism it was, already in the next edition of *Foreign Affairs* (September/October 1993), being heralded as 'The "X-article" of the post-Cold War era' (p. 26). This designation 'X-article' should be understood to mean that the article had been adopted by the government as its official political doctrine! In order to understand fully the historical significance of this, one must first look back to the period of the beginning of the Cold War. This period and its background have already been researched in great detail and it is extremely interesting to look at the similarities between the influences working behind the outer events then and those at work today.

An Anonymous Author Signs with 'X'

Looking back to the year 1947, it is possible to discern two basic features of American politics, neither of which has really changed to this day. The first is the structure of the political establishment of the United States, whose core organizations are, according to Arthur Schlesinger (historian and advisor to President Kennedy) the Carnegie, Ford and Rockefeller Foundations, the Council on Foreign Relations and its official organ, the journal *Foreign Affairs*, as well as *The New York Times*.[4] The second phenomenon is the dependence of the American Government upon the political viewpoint of the Council on Foreign Relations. Its views are worked upon by groups of specialists and then published in the periodical *Foreign Affairs* if they correspond to the propaganda aims of the Council.[5]

During 1946 and 1947 there raged a furious debate in the United States over the future of American foreign policy. In a similar way to Bill Clinton the president at the time, Harry S. Truman, was lambasted for his lack of resolve at a time of uncertainty and change. The first question was: how should the United States behave in relation to its erstwhile ally Russia? Should one give the Russians financial aid or should their imperial ambitions be thwarted? The second question ran: how can the United States help a totally devastated Western Europe? In this atmosphere of helplessness there appeared, in the July 1947 edition of *Foreign Affairs*, an article that landed like a bomb. The author of this article, which was entitled 'The Sources of Soviet Conduct', remained

anonymous, merely signing it with a mysterious 'X'. It was
here that the political strategy of 'containment' was brought
into the public domain and explained in detail. The identity
of the author was, however, soon discovered; he was George
F. Kennan, a friend of Averell Harriman and his deputy as
ambassador to Moscow during the war.[6]
    The core thoughts contained within that article were in no
way the result of one individual's insight. They were developed over many months by Harriman, Dean Acheson (later
Secretary of State), Robert Lovett (who was deputy of the
incumbent Secretary of State, George Marshall), together
with other friends. It was in private conversations and study
groups of the Council on Foreign Relations that these
thoughts were developed in greatest detail.[7]
    The result of this collective brainstorming exercise
undertaken by prominent members of the government or
professors at elite universities was only then, at the 'end of
the day', made public. All the people involved in this work
belonged to the inner echelons of the American political
establishment, some of whom were also members of secret
brotherhoods (Harriman, Lovett and the Secretary of War,
Stimson, belonged to the Skull and Bones brotherhood,
Acheson to the Scroll and Key brotherhood).[8]
    The 'X-Article' was, then, in a certain sense the result of a
group inspiration. Very shortly after its appearance, the
Truman government adopted its ideas as guiding thoughts
for its foreign policy. The first of the above-mentioned
questions was therefore to be answered with the strategy of
containment. Just like Huntington's article, the 'X-article' ran
into huge controversy. One of its sharpest critics was the
journalist Walter Lippmann, whose twelve ripostes in the
Washington Post soon appeared in the form of a book entitled
The Cold War. Thus was the era given its name. The second
question was also answered in parallel to the first by the
above personalities in the summer of 1947. Acheson and
Harriman, together with other political figures, developed

THE SOURCES OF SOVIET CONDUCT

By X

THE political personality of Soviet power as we know it today is the product of ideology and circumstances: ideology
inherited by the present Soviet leaders from the movement
in which they had their political origin, and circumstances of the
power which they now have exercised for nearly three decades in
Russia. There can be few tasks of psychological analysis more difficult than to try to trace the interaction of these two forces and
the relative rôle of each in the determination of official Soviet
conduct. Yet the attempt must be made if that conduct is to be
understood and effectively countered.

It is difficult to summarize the set of ideological concepts with
which the Soviet leaders came into power. Marxian ideology, in its
Russian-Communist projection, has always been in process of
subtle evolution. The materials on which it bases itself are extensive and complex. But the outstanding features of Communist

---

From *Foreign Affairs*, July 1947 (above)
From *Foreign Affairs*, Summer edition 1993 (below).

The Clash of Civilizations?

Samuel P. Huntington

THE NEXT PATTERN OF CONFLICT

WORLD POLITICS IS entering a new phase, and intellectuals have
not hesitated to proliferate visions of what it will be—the end of history, the return of traditional rivalries between nation states, and the
decline of the nation state from the conflicting pulls of tribalism and
globalism, among others. Each of these visions catches aspects of the
emerging reality. Yet they all miss a crucial, indeed a central, aspect
of what global politics is likely to be in the coming years.

the concept of a large-scale aid programme for Europe, later known as the Marshall Plan. Their circle was concerned to effect a rapid implementation of the aid plan, and so Harriman was appointed director of the Marshall Plan.

Isaacson and Thomas, authors of the book *The Wise Men*, have characterized the working methods of this group as follows:

> As individuals, Acheson and Harriman, Lovett and McCloy, Kennan and Bohlen, each had his blind spots and shortcomings; alone, no single one of them could have guided the country into its new role as world power. Yet collectively, this small group of men, and those who emulated their example, brought to the immense task just the right mixture of vision and practicality, aggressiveness and patience. They came together at one of those moments in history when time and place, upbringing and character, fuse into a kind of critical mass, and give ordinary men the power to forever change the way things are . . . The motives and wisdom of the old foreign policy elite can be fairly debated, but its impact is undeniable. More than any others, this small group of men made the US assume the responsibility of a world power and defined its global mission.[9]

*

The ideologists and thinkers of these groups have the task to act as middlemen between the few initiates of the West and the broad masses of the population. It is their task to formulate and then to implement the above-mentioned collective ideals. In this sense Huntington's article is merely a creative concoction of various theses that have been widely discussed since the end of the 80s (at the very latest) in the Anglo-Saxon world. Professor Huntington is himself a prominent member of these circles.[10] He is not the only one, however, who has expressed some vision of the future. In

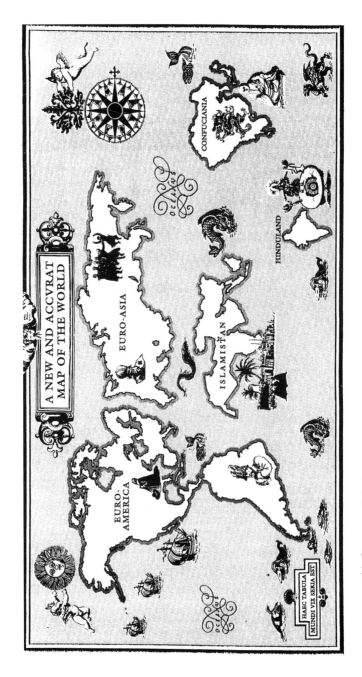

'A Survey of Defence and the Democracies' from *The Economist*, 1 September 1990.

some English and American journals such as *The Economist* and *The New York Times*, very similar ideas to Huntington's 'Clash of Civilizations' have been developed since the end of the Cold War. In *The Economist* there appeared, as early as September 1990, a map of the post-Cold War era that in many decisive aspects is extraordinarily similar to Huntington's thesis![11] Nevertheless, among the public at large, trapped in materialism, people have been searching in vain for a big idea that could encapsulate the new age after the end of the Cold War, for such people have the greatest difficulty in developing their own independent thoughts and ideas! It is here that the initiated can seize the moment. 'For there are ways and means,' says Rudolf Steiner, 'to bring into the public sphere that which from the side of the initiates one wishes to let in.'[12] It can, for example, be done through the many rituals in which the members of the Anglo-American Establishment take part. The brothers in orders such as the Skull and Bones meet weekly during their time at university and then at least twice a year thereafter, without in any way having learnt anything about occultism before. Rudolf Steiner indicated that during these rituals their etheric bodies are influenced in a very potent way. 'The consequence of which is that one can, if one so wishes, make these people into highly receptive instruments for all sorts of plans . . . for if one works on the etheric body in this way—without the person knowing it—then the understanding forces are cut off that he would otherwise possess in his intellect, if one is not able to bring understanding to the matter as we must through spiritual science.'[13]

At the beginning of the Cold War when they initiated the Marshall Plan, the so-called Wise Men were indeed *also* acting as genuine idealists. For it was probably not their *sole* aim merely to create new markets for the United States. Nonetheless, the far-reaching Americanisation of western and middle Europe has undoubtedly been one of the main consequences of this plan. This form of Americanisation perverts the true task of the West (including that of the US) and the conscious aims of many of its representatives. Huntington *also* certainly follows moral intentions. Nevertheless the central question in his article is by no means scientifically neutral such as, 'How might the new era look?' but rather 'How can the West become still more powerful?' At the end of his article this point of view emerges clearly: 'In the short term it is clearly in the interest of the West . . . to exploit differences and conflicts among Confucian and Islamic states; to support in other civilizations groups sympathetic to Western values and interests; to strengthen international institutions that reflect and legitimate Western interests and values' (pp. 48–49). It will doubtless take some time before the United States Government comes forward with a clearly articulated new doctrine, but already today many of its official utterances leave one with the impression that when that time comes the thesis of the new 'X-article' will in no way be ignored. A new American Dream for a new era?

4
A Partnership Without Peace

NATO's New Map of Europe

It was not until four years after the collapse of the Warsaw Pact that the influential western elites were able to set their initial concepts for a new world order into the form of a detailed plan. One of the results of this process was discussed and adopted as a fundamental strategy at the meeting of the NATO members' heads of government and heads of state in Brussels in January 1994. But it was difficult to avoid the impression that this was largely a case of old wine in new bottles; the strategies may have changed but the aims remained as before. With the ratification of the 'Partnership for Peace',[1] the short time of transition, which had begun with the overnight disappearance of the Iron Curtain, ended. During this time many had entertained the hope that now a 'new world order', bringing humanity peace and justice, was really possible. Particularly in the countries of middle and eastern Europe, people were, up until fairly recently, convinced that the disappearance of Bolshevism was in itself enough to bring about a considerable improvement in the situation.

Yet, as the ongoing war in the former state of Yugoslavia showed, the old demons of the past had not disappeared during the period of Communist dictatorship in eastern Europe; they were merely forgotten about. Today they are once again coming to the fore and fanning the flames of nationalism across the whole world, but most especially in the former eastern bloc. The (for many) unexpected popularity of the Russian chauvinists is due to this nationalist comeback. The slipping back into nationalism of such a militarily significant state as Russia signifies that the world is again entering an age in which old concepts such as 'balance of power' and the 'Russian danger' will, in a modified form, once more be a part of the foreign policy currency of the day.

The insider circles of the West have never really been under any illusions as to the future position adopted by the 'New Russia'. In direct contradiction to the prevailing view that Russia has become a large adopted child of the West, such circles in England and America were reckoning with the prospect of an ever-increasing tension between the West and the 'Russian Bear'. It was in this sense that *The Economist*, already on 4 December 1993, one week before the Russian elections, was warning its readers of the possible danger. In an article under the heading 'Russia resurgent: whoever wins the election on 12 December, the west faces problems', it said:

> All 13 political parties contesting the parliamentary election in Russia on 12 December agree on one thing: that Russia's power abroad must be increased ... From its role as gendarme of Europe in the nineteenth century to superpower rival in the cold war, a bossy Russia has been the norm, its recent passivity the anomaly. In the post-cold-war world, Russian interests are not likely to be identical with those of the west. One reason is that, if the world's big new fault line is to run between rich north and poor south, then Russia, which has long southern borders and a large Muslim minority, cannot ally itself unequivocally with the rich north. It must protect its 'southern' interests. In these circumstances, a western policy that assumes Russia will continue with its close Atlantic ties will be disappointed.

In other publications from the above-mentioned groups there have already been quite concrete things said about the dividing up of Europe in accordance with the old concept of zones of influence. The writers of the London-based *Foreign Report*, already on 25 November 1993, foresaw the founding of a new version of the old Slavic union between Russia, Belarus and the eastern parts of the Ukraine, though without the Baltic republics. In the same journal, on 9 December 1993, the states of the ex-eastern bloc countries were divided up into three different 'classes' according to whether they would come more under the Russian or under the western sphere of influence. Each of these three classes were supposed to play a distinct role in relation to the 'Partnership for Peace'. The 'lower class' includes all the ex-Soviet republics 'now more or less under Russia's thumb'. In Europe this class consists of Belarus and the Ukraine. The middle class includes Bulgaria, Rumania and Slovakia, 'independent and not directly threatened by Russia but given no attention at all by the West'. In the upper class were Poland, Hungary, the Czech Republic and the Baltic states.

The plan envisages a close economic and military working together between this highest category and the West. According to the authors, these countries have the best chance of being able economically and politically to reform themselves along western lines in the shortest possible time. For the lower class on the other hand there is no choice: they will increasingly fall under Russian control. The middle class will have to make do with an existence in the grey zone between the two power centres. These states will 'moulder in benign neglect until their laggardly governments and parliaments introduce badly needed economic reforms. Only then will the West take them seriously.'

Does this new tension and power constellation in Europe contain any advantages for the West? Of course it does, maintains Charles W. Maynes, chief editor of the influential journal *Foreign Policy*, writing from Washington in the journal's winter 1993 edition: 'No doubt an approach based on spheres of influence in a more democratic world would alarm those who want to see complete equality among States. But the last two decades should have taught us that any semblance of international rule of law must rest on a system that can harness the power of key States that can act.' In Europe the USA, the EU and a 'democratic' Russia should, according to Maynes, look after security and stability. In Asia this role would again fall to the United States, except this time in conjunction with Japan and China. 'Idealists and proponents of strict equality among UN members would object to a world based on spheres of influence, however benign. But the truth is that if anyone is to end military rule in Haiti, it will have to be the United States. And if someone is to end the fighting between Azerbaijanis and Armenians in Nagorno-Karabakh, it will be Russia,' writes Maynes. 'However, all these somewhat complex arguments could be better understood if one recalls the explanation already given in the beginning of his article: 'Even a superpower will exhaust itself if it tries to police the globe.'

The Ukraine Between East and West

Just how dangerous this emergence of a grey zone from the Black Sea to the Polish border can become will be clear by looking at some of the unfortunately very realistic prognoses of these Anglo-American circles.

According to these pronouncements, the western part of the Ukraine (the former Eastern Galicia) will also be a part of this grey zone. Up until 1918 this area belonged to the Austro-Hungarian monarchy and was only assigned to the Soviet Union under the terms of the Hitler-Stalin Pact in 1939; today a second splitting off of this part looks to be rather possible. Since the middle of 1993 many of the insider publications of the West have talked of an inexorable escalation in the Ukrainian crisis. The immediate cause is the catastrophic economic situation in the country. After the

'The world sends NATO back to the drawing board' from *The Economist*, 25 December 1993.

Ukraine left the rouble-zone in 1992 its currency went into free-fall. This unsettled the large Russian minority in the country (roughly 20 per cent of the 50 million inhabitants are of Russian origin) and added weight to their demands for an immediate reunification with their 'elder Slavic brother'.

Ukrainian nationalists, who live mainly in the west of the country, point at the same time to warning lessons from history. These, they argue, show that *elder brother* Russia would all-too-willingly rush to lend its *younger brother* Ukraine a helping hand. The first example of this goes back as far as the Treaty of Pereyaslavl, which was at the time (1654) understood by the Ukrainians to be an alliance between themselves and Orthodox Moscow against the Polish and Crimean allies, but which was interpreted by Moscow as making the people of Ukraine into vassals. Today then the Treaty of Pereyaslavl is held up in the Ukraine to be a classic example of how Russia will use a treaty as the prelude to an annexation.

Moscow was also not a little involved with the run-away inflation in the Ukraine, which depends on Russia for 90 per cent of its energy requirements. Moscow uses this dependency, together with the fact that the Ukraine is in debt to Russia to the tune of $900 million, as an effective means of pressure. While Moscow and the Russians living in eastern Ukraine are working for a reunification with Russia (even if this were to be initially merely a *de facto* rather than a *de jure* reunification), Ukrainian nationalists were only too willing to use the nuclear threat in order to thwart Russian hegemonic ambitions. But the atomic weapons that were stationed on their territory were not under their own direct command.

In the face of this explosive situation—which is only accentuated by further unresolved problems such as the breaking up of the Black Sea fleet—the warnings of a possible conflict between the Ukraine and Russia are not that unrealistic. At the end of November 1993 there appeared the above mentioned article in *Foreign Report* in which not only the previously touted Slavic Union was discussed but also the solution to the Ukrainian question as a whole: 'As for Ukraine, it is even possible that within a year the Russian Government will take over, in effect if not in name. Like Belarus, Ukraine would remain an "independent" state with embassies round the world and a seat at the United Nations (which both had under the Soviet Union). But all important decisions would be taken in Moscow.'

After a description of the economic crisis ('We expect Yeltsin, Grachev and Kozyrev to wait until the Ukrainian economy crashes—which could be any time—before applying more pressure for payment of oil and gas bills by suspending supplies . . . ') the prognosis becomes much more precise. Under the heading 'When the time is ripe' we read the following:

> At the right moment, with the country in a shambles, these pressures could reach a climax. At that moment the friendly 'elder brother' would move in to spare the 'younger brother' a worse fate. At this point, it is even possible that the country might split, with the eastern two-thirds, strongly Russian and imbued with Russian Orthodox Christianity, going to Russia. The capital, Kiev, which is in the eastern two-thirds, would again become the 'holy mother of Russian cities'. The western third, also known as East Galicia, might break away. . . Its religious tradition, muffled under Communism, is mainly Uniate (believers follow Orthodox ritual but are loyal to Rome). With luck the Russians might let the western Ukrainians go. But who would take them? . . . Might the West be of any help in preserving the independence of Belarus and the Ukraine? Probably not.

*

This scenario, which is full of hope for a split between Orthodox and Uniate Christians in the Ukraine, reminds one of Samuel Huntington's thesis. The Harvard professor foresees that in the future the main conflicts will be of an inter-cultural and inter-religious nature. According to his prognosis, the border between Euro-America and Euro-Asia will run straight through the Ukraine (see the map on page 58).

In view of these plans and prophecies, therefore, some of the ruling circles in the Anglo-Saxon world are now of the view that Russia should once again take up its nine-teenth-century role of policeman and control its immediate surroundings. Both the previously quoted insider prognos-tications as well as the more public 'Partnership for Peace' point in this direction. In this sense the Ukraine apparently 'ought' to break apart under the tension between its own nationalism and Russian imperialism. This then leads to the central question: do the states belonging to the 'middle-class' have any chance of surviving so long as the decadent concept of the nation state still rules the European political scene? As long as they have no understanding for concepts and ideas[2] that help to overcome this dogma, the peoples of middle and central Europe will be excellent 'partners' in the new version of the hoary old game of international tension and conflict in Europe.

5
The Balkan Politics of the International Community

Eighty Years After the Murder of the Austrian Crown Prince Franz Ferdinand

'When we heard the news from Sarajevo that the Austro-Hungarian crown prince had been brutally murdered together with his fiancé on 28 June 1914 by Serbians,' wrote Wilhelm Muehlon in the first days of August 1914, 'my first impression and my first words were: a European war is now inevitable. Austria can now only make a move, otherwise her fate is sealed ... But the traditions of the dual monarchy will ensure that that move means war.'

Wilhelm Muehlon (1878–1944), in those days a director of the steel and armaments manufacturers Krupp, was, however, one of the few central Europeans who understood the situation at the beginning of this century and had a sense for the forces at work in history. His contemporaries were more or less completely blind to this reality, or at best naive. In his recognition of the ever-pressing need to reform the already decadent Habsburg monarchy, the young idealist and humanist Muehlon was almost completely alone. 'The annexation of Bosnia and Hercegovina [effected by Austria in 1908] was already a great mistake and the cause of much friction,' he wrote. 'The fact that the Serbs rile against it is wholly understandable. Had one promised the Serbs their territory, at least the one in which fellow Serbs were living then, Austro-Hungary would undoubtedly have created a grateful friend in an enlarged Serbia, who would have better protected and strengthened the position of the dual monarchy in the Balkans than the Austro-Hungarian policy of conquest could do.'[1]

Reading the writings of Muehlon on the fateful summer of 1914 from our present-day vantage point leaves one with the definite impression that, despite everything, in central Europe at that time there were the right people with the requisite insight into events. But people like Muehlon and Helmuth von Moltke were unable to break through at the political level. The locomotive of Austrian and German foreign policy was at that time so preoccupied and blinded by power intrigues that the already strained relations between the peoples of central Europe and the southern Slavs led inexorably towards a violent confrontation. The Austrian ultimatum to Serbia of July 1914, which was certainly intended as a declaration of war, can really be described as a trap—artfully designed (partly by Austria herself) to bring about Austria's downfall—into which Austria fell headlong.[2]

The fact that certain occult circles in the Anglo-American West, as well as the Catholic Church, had been consciously preparing for a conflict between the Germanic regions and the Slavs at least since the end of the nineteenth century only goes to highlight the tragic ignorance of the true central European impulses of the time. For indeed, at that time truly realistic and appropriate ideas were coming not only from anthroposophical spiritual science. Such thoughts would have shown themselves to be of the greatest possible practical value, if only they had been taken seriously. That the slumbering spiritual and moral potential in central Europe could have come into its own was, for example, described by Wilhelm Muehlon when, on the eve of the First World War, he gloomily registered the mood in Germany and Austria: 'One would no doubt be laughed at if one said that a state can actually grow smaller in territorial size while at the same time growing much bigger and influential; the point is not the brute force possessed by any nation, but its moral level that is unconquerable so long as it is of a higher nature.'[3]

*

Eighty years have now elapsed since the murder of Arch-
duke Franz Ferdinand. The Balkans are still consumed by
war. No one any longer expects superpower politics from
Austria to solve the apparently intractable conflicts. At least
in western and central Europe, one looks to the 'victorious
powers' in the Cold War for any such solutions. And yet,
since the end of 1993, the Balkan policies of the world's
single remaining superpower have been heavily criticized.
Thus Charles Krauthammer (one of Washington's leading
journalists) undoubtedly speaks for many when, in an unusually sharp article, he says that 'the central idea of Clinton's
foreign policy' is defined by the fact 'that in the post-Cold
War era the US can shed its arduous international re-
sponsibilities by transferring them to the UN or sundry
other multilateral constructions'. Despite the convenient
excuses which always seem to be to hand in the event of
possible failures, says Krauthammer, the policy of the Clinton
administration is leading to continuous and unnecessary
humiliation for America.[4]

In the European NATO, member states' politicians are
blamed and attacked for merely playing with words while
in reality doing nothing against the Serbian aggressors.
When a few merely symbolic bombs were twice dropped
on Serb positions by NATO war planes, it was immediately pointed out that here it 'was in both cases *American*
pilots who had taken the initiative' as Josef Joffe wrote in
the *Süddeutsche Zeitung*. 'Although Bosnia in no way lies in
the Rocky Mountains, the Europeans just seem to lack the
courage or the team-spirit.'[5] In America the talk is more
that not just America but the West as a whole has no
strategy or policy for 'the Bosnian conflict'. This is summarized by Krauthammer as follows: 'At root the problem is

not personalities [i.e. politicians] *but ideas.'*

The criticism reached a peak with the shelling of the town of Gorazde by the Serbs in April 1994. After the NATO ultimatum in February which eased the siege around Sarajevo, and after the treaty for a Federation of the Bosnian Muslims and Croats was signed in Washington, the struggle began for the small town of Gorazde, then overflowing with refugees. The Bosnian Serbs had been pounding the so-called UN safety zone of Gorazde for three weeks, unconcerned by the feeble American air strikes; they knew that Paris and London were too worried about their own UN troops to give the go-ahead for a real military intervention. Apart from this, Milosevic, Karadzic and other 'Serbian patriots' understood only too well how to manipulate for their own ends the US-Russian relationship with its constant oscillations between conflict and co-operation. When the Serb tanks rolled into Gorazde on 15 April 1994 and the whole world—shocked by the ever-intensifying bombardment of the civil population—was waiting for NATO intervention, President Clinton placated the aggressors: one wished to act 'decisively but not provocatively' and try not to upset the military balance.

*

Is it really true that the politicians in the West (which today means in the EU and the United States) really have no ideas, no concept for the Balkans? Is it really the case that all the moves on the part of the West between the beginning of the war around 28 June 1991 and June 1994 have merely been improvisation? A closer look at the western engagement during this time reveals quite another picture. This became clear during Clinton's visit to Paris at the beginning of June 1994; suddenly his host was more than pleased with the new American position on Bosnia. In January the American president was still rejecting the proposal from Paris and

London for partition of Bosnia-Hercegovina, saying that it
would be a reward for Serbian aggression. Now, however,
he pledged himself to putting 'the whole of America's
weight' behind the 'new' 51:49 partition plan. The French
believed him and with good reason.

What is the meaning of this oscillation in American policy?
Had President Clinton's position in relation to the Balkan
war changed so radically? One has reason to doubt that it
had. Clinton's new strategy expressed exactly the line that
American policy has been following since the beginning of
the war, but which until now has been undeclared. If the
West has problems with its Balkan policy they are certainly
not of a conceptual nature. It is rather that American policy
makers are having problems with their voters; in other
words they have a propaganda problem. The influence of
the electronic media in the last few years has created a
troublesome new imperative for politicians everywhere:
they are now continuously forced to explain their actions to
their voters. This is especially the case in America. The
problem for them here is that the actual direction of their
policies often stands in direct contradiction to their stated
aims. This discrepancy shows itself most strongly in the case
of their Balkan policy: they wish to show themselves to be
acting out of moral precepts, but they cannot, in the case of
the Balkans, hide their true intentions for very long.

For the leading circles in the West and the Catholic Church,
the Balkan war offers a good opportunity to further their
long-term aims. Unlike the politicians of central Europe,
who, as always, have simply been ignorant of actual historical impulses, these circles manipulate events precisely on
the basis of their understanding of such impulses. A symptom of this is the fact that Clinton, as Jim Hoagland (a
columnist for the *Washington Post*) describes, despite all
vacillations of American foreign policy in other areas, at
least has his firm grasp on Russia. The public are only as
disappointed as they are by the handling of international

From the article by Samuel P. Huntington in *Foreign Affairs*,
Summer edition 1993.

crises (according to Jim Hoagland) because the White House
does not make clear the long-term aims of its foreign policy.
The key element of this successful policy has been the
influence it has exerted upon the development of Russia.[6]

It is also the opinion of Hoagland that one needs to
observe the 'results' of the policies of these circles rather
than the phrases used by politicians. The above-named
occult circles wish to reconstitute the ancient East-West
border. The fact that this border runs straight through
Bosnia is one of the deepest causes of the present tragedy. In
the West it is desired to control the cultural and spiritual
development of the eastern Slavs, for it is known that among
them the next cultural epoch will unfold. The possibilities,
however, that would be opened up by a peaceful coexistence
in this area are regarded as especially dangerous by these
circles. For through a mutual fructification of the cultures
of eastern and middle Europe there would arise a real
alternative to the unstated aims of the western circles: it is
precisely here in the Balkans that real universal culture
could arise that would *spiritually* overcome the ethnic principle and could serve to support the development of a true
individualism. Then a whole stream of civilization would
arise that would endanger both the position of Catholicism
in central Europe and the Anglo-Saxon influence in eastern
Europe. It is just this that they wish at all costs to prevent
from happening.

Against this background, then, one can begin to understand why the so-called ethnic conflict in the former
Yugoslavia is not that unhelpful to some of the power
brokers in western and southern Europe. These circles
have reached an unofficial agreement over their respective spheres of influence. The border between the western
and central European region, where the old Catholic element is to exercise spiritual domination through the
mentality inside the bureaucratism of the EU, and the
East that is to come under Anglo-Saxon domination, runs

straight through the Balkans. This war has served as a useful catalyst for the achievement of these goals. Because it is, however, impossible to speak of such plans without appearing immoral in the extreme, there arise, from time to time, some very difficult questions for the UN officers in charge of the Bosnian aid operations and military with respect to international policy in the Balkans. Such officers—recently they have tended to be French—have then quickly lost their posts. On the other hand, some sections of the Serbian economy have been thriving, not least thanks to huge imports of fuel that have been supplied via the Italian Mafia.

The quickest and most decisive action taken by the Americans during the three years of the war was their—so far successful—dictation of a Muslim-Croat alliance. Yet this new 'federation' is in reality simply the attempt to create a greater Croatia. The achievement of this aim would remove the last obstacles preventing the final determination of the long prepared for border. As a self-sufficient cultural unity the Bosnian Muslims would otherwise be able to form a bridging middle element, something that would be very unpleasant for certain influential circles. Therefore it was necessary to move quickly to counter such a danger.

*

'America cannot solve every problem and must not become the world's policeman,' declared Clinton on 4 March 1994 in a 'World Wide Forum' in CNN. Yet at the same time he upheld the 'unconditional leadership role' of the US on the global stage. Such statements confuse both politicians and ordinary people. Clinton has had to react negatively, and without adequate explanation, to the demands of the American Congress and Senate for a suspension of the one-sided arms embargo against the Bosnian Muslims. He was actually helped in this by the Russian foreign minister who made Russia's opposition to such a move clear: 'If the US deny the norms of human rights,' said Kozyrev on 14 June 1994 after a meeting with Radovan Karadzic in Moscow, 'then this could worsen the whole international climate and could even lead to a third world war!'

That such voices are to be heard in Washington and Moscow exactly 80 years after the murder in Sarajevo and three years after the outbreak of the present Balkan war is certainly no coincidence. One increasingly hears today that this war 'should really be over and done with soon' or else the French and the British will have to withdraw their troops. Such statements reveal the desire and the intention to perform once again an act of great historical consequence in the Balkans: the 'peaceful' sealing of the old-and-new East-West demarcation line in southern Europe.

6
Masaryk's World Revolution and the Social Configuration of Europe

Illusionism on the Way to Apocalyptic Times

Almost 80 years after the last ultimatum to the Serbs, an historical circle was completed for Europe on 22 April 1994. The NATO ultimatum to the Bosnian Serbs, which like its predecessor in 1914 was actually directed at the Belgrade leadership (and Slobodan Milosevic in particular), merely demonstrated how helplessly the politicians of today act when confronted by the major challenges of our age. Once again recourse was made to the use of force, which was both inappropriate and would probably also have been unnecessary if the real causes of the conflict had been recognized early enough. Once again some people in Europe turned to the old solution of trying to solve conflicts by the creation of new nation states, although two world wars have already shown that this in no way addresses the underlying problems. For the real question lying behind the conflicts of the twentieth century is: 'What would a "new world order" that is in *true* keeping with the spirit of the times look like and how could it be brought about?'

In January 1991, as the bombs were raining down on Baghdad, the American president George Bush announced his temporarily last version of the new world order. His conception was greeted with much acclaim and excitement, both in Europe and the United States. The actual plan, however, contained no new ideas; it reaffirmed the principle of national self-determination and held up the United Nations as the centre of the international community of democratic nations. It was almost a replay of the 1919 Versailles Peace Conference! Yet, 75 years later, there was again a war raging in the Balkans and a nationalistic Balkanization of central and eastern Europe was a distinct possibility, due in part to the very real fears in these regions of Moscow's imperialistic ambitions. The need for a *true* new order for the world is therefore certainly impossible to refute. By means of an historical example taken from the first half of the twentieth century, we shall in what follows be looking at how those Europeans who considered themselves to be bearers of the true democratic ideal perceived this need. We shall also be looking at what parallels can be drawn with the present situation.

*

It is not often that a single personality embodies the thoughts and feelings of a whole generation to such an all-encompassing extent as Thomas Garrigue Masaryk. Masaryk (1850–1937) was the spiritual father, the founder and, for a long time, the president of Czechoslovakia. Above all in his writings, in which he speaks about the beginning of a new world era, he brought to expression the hopes and aspirations of many of his European contemporaries. After the First World War he was seen as *the* prophet of a democratic and humanistic renewal of Europe. Also more recently, during the Prague Spring of 1968 and the Velvet Revolution of 1989, many Czechs experienced his ideas on the nature of the state like a ray of light amidst the darkness and general dearth of any new ideas.

The chief interests of Masaryk the professor of philosophy lay outside the confines of his subject. 'I have never thought of myself as a philosopher, still less as a metaphysicist,' he once said when questioned about his teaching at the university.[1] Since his early youth he had concerned himself far more with social and political questions. As the son of a

Slovak coachman and a Moravian mother, who came originally from German-speaking territory, he grew up in the
Moravian part of Slovakia and felt himself to be a Slovak
through and through. Although coming from a simple
family, his talents and his father's work at the house of an
aristocratic family enabled him to gain access to books and
education. During the 1860s Masaryk studied in Vienna
where the philosopher Franz Brentano was teaching at the
time. Masaryk was to say later that Brentano, both as a
teacher and as a human being, 'had had the greatest influence upon me'. Despite his enthusiasm for the ideals of
democracy he developed a particularly deep connection to
Plato's world-view. It was at that time that he first discovered his own national identity. He was for a while chairman
of the council of the Czech Academic Association and wrote
his first article in the Czech language on the subject of Plato's
love for his fatherland.[2]

In 1882 Masaryk was called to Prague where a Czech
university was being founded at the behest of the Czech
members of the parliament in Vienna. At first the young
Slovak professor had quite a problem with the Czech language and initially he had to have his writings corrected.
This did not stop him from holding lively discussions in
his seminars on the contemporary situation of the Czech
people. He was anything but a chauvinist. His desire to learn
about the peoples of Europe had led him at an early age to
study French, Russian, Italian and English. German was his
mother tongue. At the university Masaryk made a detailed
study of the history of Czech politics after 1848 and brought
the results of his studies together in the book *The Czech
Question* (1895). Following the victory of the Young Czech
party in the elections of 1891 he became a member of the
Viennese parliament. From then on he was also a politician.
More than 30 years later, after the First World War when the
Czech-dominated Czechoslovakia was born, Rudolf Steiner
said of Masaryk that it was one of the deepest symptoms of

the times that 'such a truly significant figure as Masaryk
now stands at the head of the Czechoslovakian Republic for
he himself is a Slovak . . . a true Slovak'.[3]

Masaryk's burning interest in politics was the result of his
extreme sensitivity for the challenges of his times, which
were marked by the ending of Kali Yuga and the beginning
of a new Michaelic Age. He described what had moved him
his whole life long in the following words:

> The crisis of modern humanity is of an all-encompassing
> nature, a crisis affecting the whole human being, the
> whole spiritual life: the whole of modern life, all institu-
> tions, all world-views need revising; the lack of whole-
> ness, the fragmentation of modern man and his life, the
> fragmentation and lack of wholeness in society and the
> general spiritual anarchy, the battle between the present
> and the past, the battle between fathers and sons . . .
> permeates the whole culture. We all search for inner peace
> of soul, but how and where can we find it? In the search for
> spiritual peace many fall into the trap of an exaggerated
> individualism and subjectivism, and it is from this that the
> moral and spiritual isolation stems; many give them-
> selves over to materialism and mechanization . . . even
> though they are convinced that a permanent ordering of
> society is not possible without a general agreement upon
> some kind of world-view; many people revolt against the
> churches only to become the slave of political parties and
> their factions. It is said that to speak of and to promote
> morality is to fall for an old-fashioned moralizing, while
> belief and religious life are condemned as superstition.
> Restlessness, discontent, scepticism, tiredness from inner
> conflict, pessimism, anger and doubt: all end in suicide,
> militarism and war. These are the shadows of modern life,
> of the modern human being . . .[4]

Masaryk was convinced that a new order must be found

for Europe, an order that corresponded to the needs of humanity in the twentieth century. The main aim of this essential development was for him the democratization of all political systems and the freeing of all the peoples of the Habsburg Empire from Austrian hegemony. Over time he became convinced that the greatest obstacle in the way of a humanitarian and democratic central Europe lay in the ageing monarchical structures of Germany and Austria. And because these great powers did not have the will to bring about a peaceful process of reform the change would probably have to come through a revolution. Thus when the First World War broke out in 1914 the pacifist and humanitarian Masaryk decided to use all means possible to bring about the downfall of the Habsburg monarchy. He immediately understood that the economic strength of the West would determine the outcome of the war. But it was essentially his belief in the western ideal of democracy and its anchoring in a nation state on the French model that made him a natural supporter of the Allies. He regarded these two political ideals as the panacea for all problems of the age.

'In contradistinction to Germany and Austria, the Allies accepted the modern principle of nationality for all peoples and supported the cause of small states and nations,' wrote Masaryk after the war. '... By accepting the principle of nationality, the Allies guarded themselves against chauvinism. True, Germany too was "national", though she conceived her "nationality" as something superior to the "nationality" of others.' Masaryk believed that he had found the explanation for this in the German fallback from the liberalism of the nineteenth century to the cult of the Roman-German Caesarism: 'The humanitarian ideals of Lessing, Herder, Goethe, Kant and Schiller, which arose out of western and universal world development and were created out of collaboration with this course of development, were replaced by a Pan-

German imperialism . . . Germany nurtured the ideal of the Roman Empire also geographically. The ideal of the West, on the other hand, is directed at the organization of humanity as a whole—above all at the connection between Europe and America and with them the remaining parts of the world and humanity: an extensive and intensive humanitarianism.'[5]

*

Thomas Masaryk, as we have seen, was one of the leading intellectuals of his time who believed that humanity in the twentieth century was being called upon to enact radical and far-reaching changes. Nonetheless, despite all his academic education he did not understand the true background to this monumental 'crisis of modern humanity'. To all appearances he therefore rejected Rudolf Steiner's spiritual science, the existence of which he undoubtedly knew. 'I have observed again and again that many people,' he wrote, 'even those educated in science, fall for the most varied forms of mysticism, spiritualism and occultism, but is such an increase in religiosity to be desired?'[6] When, during Masaryk's later presidency, Ludwig Polzer-Hoditz proposed to him some anthroposophical social reforms he did indeed show interest[7] but the spiritual-scientific origins of the proposals remained ultimately alien to him.

One of the main motifs from these origins shall now be considered in greater detail. For only against this background can one understand why a truly *new* world order is really so urgently needed today. In his book *Knowledge of the Higher Worlds* Rudolf Steiner has described the form of initiation appropriate for the individual in our time. Some of the stages of development described in this book can, however, be applied, of course in a somewhat altered form, to humanity *as a whole*. Rudolf Steiner described, for example, a characteristic collective process: that during the course of the fifth post-Atlantean epoch humanity as a whole crosses the threshold not as a single pupil of higher knowledge who experiences his initiation fully consciously, but as a community and unconsciously. A direct result of this is something which affects society as a whole, namely, what Steiner calls 'the splitting of the personality', a process in which the originally harmonious interaction of the soul forces of thinking, feeling and willing falls apart.

In the case of humanity as a whole these soul qualities correspond to the three areas of social life: the spiritual life, the life of rights, and the economic life. While these three areas originally functioned as a harmonious unity within the social organism, they are now all seeking to realize a maximum degree of independence for themselves. A few hundred years ago these three areas of human existence were inseparable, but in the course of the fifth post-Atlantean epoch a rapid and thorough-going change in human consciousness is occurring. With the unconscious crossing of the threshold there began a huge advance in the pace of technological development, the ultimate goal of which is to unite humanity in a common economic system. On the other hand, however, human beings are still connected to certain folk groups and geographic regions and so feel themselves to be threatened by this hegemonic drive towards a world economy. This is an example of the disintegrating nature of the social impulses of humanity.[8]

Masaryk felt above all the strong impulses of the folk culture (or spiritual life) on the one side and the less conscious impulse of the rights life to free itself from the old structures. As we have already seen, he did not regard himself as a philosopher. He could indeed clearly feel the existential crisis of modern humanity everywhere but was unable to sufficiently penetrate these feelings with any systematic and consequential thinking. An example of this is the fact that he campaigned particularly strongly for the rights of self-determination for all peoples, even the smallest, within the Habsburg Empire without having thought through at all the problems that would result from such a policy.

Led by his idealistic strivings Masaryk believed the First World War offered him a one-time opportunity to found what he felt could be a just state. Originally this task, in his opinion, had lain with Austria. But since the old monarchy had been unable to transform itself into a multi-national confederation of autonomous peoples, the task had now passed over to the Czech people.[9] Right from the beginning, however, Masaryk did not simply plan a pure Czech state based on the territory of the historical Bohemia; rather he pressed for the union of the 'historical lands' of Bohemia, Moravia and Lower Silesia (or the Czech region) with Slovakia.

The concept of a people's 'right to self-determination' provided an extremely powerful propaganda weapon for the Czechs to fight the war with. By using the argument that the Austrians would certainly not provide this 'natural right' of the smaller nationalities within the Empire they were able to persuade the Americans to continue the war until the Austro-Hungarians had been completely beaten. Masaryk was quite open about this: 'When I arrived in America (1918) I found that there were still everywhere strong feelings of friendliness towards Austria, which we had to work hard to combat . . . The Americans had to be persuaded that our nation desired to be free and would fight for its freedom. We were always being told that the Czech leaders at home did not pose as enemies of Austria. We had to contradict that notion . . . Our propaganda everywhere had the aim of familiarizing Americans with our political and cultural history. They knew about the Czechs and the former Kingdom of Bohemia, but we had problems with the Slovaks; they were unknown and the Americans found it hard to conceive that they formed a part of our nation.'[10]

Thomas Garrigue Masaryk (1850-1937).

Even the Slovaks only understood this with difficulty. It took the Pittsburg agreement (30 May 1918) to convince them. In this agreement their full autonomy was guaranteed. Masaryk was thus able to persuade them to join with the Czechs and so form the state of Czechoslovakia. Later, however, he conceded that he had no clear idea of what the concept of the 'right of self-determination' actually meant: 'In fact this right . . . had not until now been clearly formulated,' he wrote in 1925. 'Did it apply to the whole nation or also to parts of nations? A minority, even a larger one, is not a nation . . . The autonomy of the whole and the part are not only determined in accordance with one's own rights but also in accordance with the rights of others, and *autonomy is always and everywhere affected not only by considerations of nationality and language, but also by economic factors among others* [author's italics]'.[11]

In reality then the Czecho-Slovak bipolarity after the war developed into a caricature of the Austro-Hungarian duality. For although this new multi-ethnic nation[12] withstood the economic crises of the 20s and 30s relatively well, preserved its parliamentary democracy and within a short period of time built more than 3,000 Slovak middle and high schools, the enthusiasm of the Slovaks—who had been so eagerly courted—soon turned into discontent. This was not least due to the fact that Masaryk had actually broken his Pittsburg promise. It became quite clear that he had never for a moment thought of granting the Slovaks genuine autonomy. His 'humanistic Czechoslovakia' revealed itself to be a rigorously centralized state in which minorities were systematically out-voted. At the latest by 1933 this new state was beginning to come apart through external and internal pressures. It thus came as no surprise when Slovakia declared independence on 6 October 1938, one year after the death of Masaryk, and a week after the annexation of the Sudetenland by Hitler's Germany.

*Central Europe's Failure and the 'Small' Apocalypse
at the end of the Twentieth Century*

The example of Masaryk is intended to serve here as a symptom of the mentality and actions of an educated elite of central European humanists and democrats who fought against the surviving remnants of the old monarchical structures during the first third of this century. (Masaryk himself described this form of government in its decadence as 'Czarism'.) They failed, however, in their attempt to provide a truly appropriate form for social renewal due to their fixation on the idol of the concept of the nation state as originally inspired by the French. Masaryk and his followers saw the First World War as a 'world revolution', but they did not understand that the new states of central Europe would only have been able to develop into true democracies if they had limited themselves to the ordering of the 'rights' life, while giving over economic questions to a kind of independent commission, and education policy to free individual initiatives. Only in such circumstances would it have been possible for Masaryk's humanistic aims to be realized.

It was, then, a tragic failure for central Europe when people such as Masaryk failed to appreciate the difference between the legitimate striving of their peoples for cultural autonomy on the one hand and the place of a multi-cultural democratic life of rights within the social sphere of humanity on the other. Instead they strove for the strongest political hegemony of *their* own people on *their* territory. This was tragic, because it is just in central Europe that there is a very special predisposition to separate the life of rights out from folk impulses. The late emergence of the nation states in central Europe and the tendency towards federalism there can be seen as symptoms of this basic disposition. According to Rudolf Steiner, the central European lives particularly intensively in 'all that pertains to the legal [life of rights], democratic and state element in the social organism'.[13] It is therefore the task of central Europe to find new forms for the state activity within the social organism.

   In the same way as central Europe has a special predisposition for the development of federal structures, the West possesses a particular predisposition for the development of the economic system. Or, in the words of Rudolf Steiner, 'If the economic member of the social organism is to be built up then one must learn from the West, from figures such as Thomas Reid, John Stuart Mill, Buckle, Adam Smith and so on.'[14] The preconditions for the development of the independent economic sphere of humanity in the form of a world-encompassing economic organism was developed by Great Britain during the course of the nineteenth century. What is noteworthy here is the Industrial Revolution and the development of an international trading network by the British Navy and merchant marine. In the twentieth century leadership in this area passed to the United States, inasmuch as they initiated reductions in international tariffs and trade restrictions (GATT or WTO) and considerably speeded up the pace of trade through the development of air transport.

   Today the Anglo-American West also seeks to solve the problem of nationalities and yet it does not possess the necessary natural predisposition for this task. In the West one thinks primarily in economic terms. Thus the American voices that concern themselves with the nationalities question sound rather as if they are out of their depth. They give a diagnosis but do not know how to apply the correct treatment: 'From Haiti in the western hemisphere to the remnants of Yugoslavia in Europe, from Somalia, Sudan and Liberia in Africa to Cambodia in South-east Asia, a disturbing new phenomenon is emerging: the failed nation-state, utterly incapable of sustaining itself as a member of the international community'—such was the diagnosis given in a much-noted essay by two American diplomats.[15]

The real problem is that the life of rights is unable to establish itself in a healthy way. Therefore what we experience today is its cruel caricature: chauvinistic separatism. The nationalistic currency and customs policies that go along with this enforce unnecessary restrictions on the economic life that is seeking to encompass the whole earth. And since modern economics can only function on a large scale, the large economic blocs of North America, Japan, Europe, and soon probably China as well, find themselves in a conflict between nationalism and imperialism, and because of their limitations these blocs also only present a grotesque counter-image of a true, socially just, global economics. In the final analysis, the Russian imperialism since the beginning of this century is also really just a caricature of this striving to unite the whole world under one economic system. Bolshevism was a militant economic ideology (Communism was its costume) that attempted to subordinate all other social forces to the economy. If one considers the situation today more closely one comes to the conclusion that the spiritual life cannot develop itself as an independent entity as long as the two counter-forces of true social renewal—nationalism and imperialism—are fighting against each other.[16] This is why the healthy and independent development of the rights life on the one side and of the economic sphere on the other side is so necessary.

*

When Rudolf Steiner spoke in September 1924 about the apocalyptic nature of events in the twentieth century, and especially the end of the century, he spoke among other things of the danger that would arise of the increasing power of the 'group factor' which acts against the real tendency of the times (which is to unfold the free individuality). Both 'large groups' and 'small groups' would be

subjected to dangerous seductions and 'must be lifted out
of the danger in which they find themselves'. Steiner
pointed to the fact that the small groups correspond to Gog
in the imaginative language of the writer of the Apocalypse
of St John whereas the larger are called 'Magog'. He added
that the anti-individualistic seduction of these groups had
the aim of bringing about the apocalyptic battle of Gog
and Magog:

> But people are not at all disposed to develop real
> understanding in this area. This could be observed when
> the first attempt to counter what is to come in the future—
> the seductions of Gog and Magog—was made by means
> of the movement for the threefold social organism, which
> was an attempt to lead things along a course that would
> turn out best for humanity. The idea of the threefold social
> organism would have been able to lead humanity across
> the threshold, but the way in which the idea was received
> shows just what enormous dangers lie ahead for human-
> ity in relation to these things.[17]

It must be emphasized here that as a rule the apocalyptic
pronouncements of Steiner do not apply until the far distant
future (see the Nuremberg lectures of 1908[*]). Nonetheless a
kind of foretaste or preview of these events is already
happening in our times.

In the history of the twentieth century one can find many
examples of these seductions of larger and smaller groups.
The above-mentioned perversion of human soul forces which
are seeking independence is certainly among the most prominent of these phenomena. An example of the one-sided
increase and seductive power of the Magog forces was the
division of the world into two ruling blocs (East and West)

---

[*] Rudolf Steiner, *The Apocalypse of St John*, Rudolf Steiner Press,
London 1977.

between 1945 and 1989. Up until 1945 one knew only of various historical *great powers* but after Europe had been inwardly and outwardly ruined by National Socialism there arose two *superpowers*. And behind these superpowers with their imperialistic aims lay two different economic doctrines, Communism and capitalism. Their struggle for world hegemony arose therefore out of the economic sphere but, through the temptation of the Magog forces, expanded out to include the whole social life of the peoples in their respective spheres of influence. As a consequence, the Gog forces that tempt smaller groups into nationalism had been, at least on the surface, pushed into the background. This was also the case in Czechoslovakia. The years between the Communist *putsch* of 1948 and the turning-point of 1989 were relatively quiet in respect of tensions between Czechoslovaks and Russians on the one side and Czechs and Slovaks on the other. The single exception to this was the Prague Spring of 1968.

After the 'Velvet Revolution' of 1989 the rights life and the economic life of humanity developed further apart. Once again the powers of Gog and Magog influence events: with respect to the latter we can see how the influence of the American economy has since expanded across the globe, while the Gog forces show themselves in numerous smaller countries in the form of a chauvinistic national wave. And again, as in the time of Rudolf Steiner, the middle has failed. In Germany one did not, during reunification, distinguish between the economic and rights life; economic reunification, which was justifiable and necessary, was extended into the political realm, and almost nobody thought about offering the lands of East Germany a continued autonomy. Thus was thrown away the one chance to strengthen the federalism in middle Europe which had already been weakened over the years. All the political forces in eastern Germany who were in favour of such aims were quickly silenced. Today in Germany the undifferentiated way in which the three spheres (economic, spiritual and rights) are regarded is damaging all three. In this way there arises an anti-culture, or non-culture, which manifests itself on the one hand in the anti-social tendencies of the market economy and on the other in an increasingly less democratic and centralized national patriotism in the French style.

These symptoms also quickly showed themselves in the smaller countries of central Europe. In Czechoslovakia, for example, there was no withstanding nationalistic seduction. In January 1993 the Czechs and the Slovaks separated from each other; Masaryk's vision of a multi-ethnic state was finally shattered. Despite this, though, many people today still believe in his 'world illusion' that 'the democratic ideal . . . is not just politically . . . but also economically fruitful'.[18] This means falling for the naive illusion that all the problems of the modern world can be solved *simply* by turning to democracy.[19] However, now the pendulum between Gog and Magog has swung in the other direction. The newly-awakened Russian imperialism now seems to be in a position to threaten the newly independent 'small groups' in eastern central Europe. Until the social life of humanity can be established on the basis of a threefold harmony, the history of Europe will to a very large extent continue to be determined by similar movements of this pendulum.

7

The Changing Face of Europe: Part One

'Solidarity'

Warsaw, 1 August 1994. It is unusually hot and the guards of honour in the Pilsudski Square are finding it hard going. From time to time one of the guards falls out of his row and collapses onto the cool grass where a nurse tends to him with towels and mineral water. Nonetheless, despite the tropical temperatures of up to 40° C, the fact that there is no shade at all and that they are in heavy uniform and have to wear enormous boots, it is not the guards who have the most difficult role to play on the fiftieth anniversary of the Warsaw uprising. There are some difficult questions to be answered. Did the Polish Resistance fight in vain against the Nazis and the Bolsheviks? Was the uprising 'an escape from two giants'? Were the 16,000 dead rebels and 150,000 civilians who were brutally murdered during the 63 days of the uprising the sacrificial victims of a political miscalculation by their government? And why did the western Allies stand idly by while the infamous SS brigades 'Rona' and 'Dirlewanger' (which consisted of collaborators and criminals) mercilessly carried out Himmler's commands to raise the city to the ground and kill 'all Poles living in Warsaw without any regard for their age or sex'? The Polish historian P. Jasienica says simply 'the Warsaw uprising was militarily directed against the Germans and politically against the Russians but ended up actually being against the Poles'.

In contrast to this debate, which once again erupted among historians and journalists during the build up to the commemorations—for the first time taking place against the

backdrop of a free and democratic Poland—the Catholic
Church and Lech Walesa confidently proclaimed that the
uprising naturally was no act of national stupidity; Solidarity, the independent trade union in a totalitarian state, was
the continuation and the fruit of this heroic uprising. From
the Vatican itself there came the confirmative message from
Pope John Paul II for the celebratory mass on 1 August: 'We
can only silently bow our heads in the face of the price that
that generation paid 50 years ago for the *independence of their
homeland* [author's italics].'[1]

*

In the years 1943–44, when it was already clear who the
victors would be, the 'Polish question' was one of the most
difficult subjects regularly discussed by the Allies. The
exiled Polish government in London was too independent
and too unsympathetic towards Communism. That is what
Churchill and Roosevelt heard from Stalin at the first of the
conferences of the 'Big Three' in Teheran. But the Americans
and the English had recognized this democratically inclined
government for a long time and maintained full diplomatic
relations with it.

It was not, however, in 1943 that Poland first became the
focus of the biggest European war of all time. Already in
1939 the Polish question had stood, diplomatically, at the
centre of a kind of overture of the coming war. In response
to the Polish Government's feeling in March that year of
being threatened by Hitler's naked territorial ambitions,
Britain and France promised to guarantee the security of
the Polish borders, and later gave weight to their promises
by concluding treaties with Poland. When the Germans
invaded on 1 September, and Stalin unleashed his war
machine from the East, Poland's western 'allies' had already
left her in the lurch. Nevertheless, two days later, France and
Britain declared war on the Third Reich. The Second World

War actually began in Poland. And already in this beginning one could see some of the symptoms that were to be played out in the behaviour of the main actors in the tragedy of 1944 and its consequences.

*

At the beginning of 1944 the Red Army was on the offensive. By January its first units had pushed across the Polish border against the Germans. But some diplomatic circles of the West, particularly in the United States, were worried. It was election year in America and the public wanted to be told about the president's long-term war plans. Averell Harriman was the new American ambassador to Moscow at the time and he reported that already at the conference in Teheran Roosevelt had mentioned his problems with the American voters to Stalin ('I have six million voters of Polish origin'); they would, he had said, definitely not consider Poland to be a liberated country after the war if it held no free elections. 'Roosevelt . . . allowed Stalin to assume that the Atlantic Charter's idealistic proclamations against spheres of influence [by which were meant especially the Sovietization of Poland—A.R.] were mainly for domestic political consumption and would not be used to prevent the Soviets from imposing "friendly" regimes along their periphery.'[2]

During the post-war years Averell Harriman always maintained that at that time he had really believed that the Kremlin was interested in a democratic Polish government. The sole requirement that Stalin put forward then was that he wished to have 'friendly neighbours' in Warsaw. In his published memoirs Harriman writes that he saw the diplomacy of the exiled Czech president Beneš as the best model for a reasonable solution to the Polish question. Eduard Beneš, the closest ally of Thomas Masaryk at the time of the founding of Czechoslovakia, went to Moscow from the London base of the Czechoslovakian Government at the end

Churchill, Roosevelt, Stalin, Averell Harriman (far right, above) at the Crimea Conference in the town of Yalta (February 1945).

of 1943 and concluded an alliance with Moscow that promised the full reconstitution of his state. American diplomats had hoped for a similar development for the exiled Polish Government and had believed Stalin's guarantee for free elections after the end of the war, so Harriman assures us.[3]

Harriman's unpublished notes from this time, however, reveal a quite different picture. It is only in the last few years that his private archive has been opened up to researchers (the Harriman papers are deposited in the US Library of Congress) and one of the first results of this has been the comprehensive documentation on *Harriman and the Polish Question* by William Larsh, a lecturer at Yale University.[4] According to Larsh's research: 'Harriman was more than just an important intermediary between Moscow and Washington—when he took up his post as US ambassador to Russia in October 1943 he was granted virtual *carte blanche* to conduct American foreign policy in that part of the world.'[5] 'His concern in early 1944 over the absence of an early settlement for Poland was not motivated by any deep-seated fear of Soviet ambitions for *total* domination of its western neighbour,' quotes Larsh from an unpublished study of Harriman in Moscow. '. . . Harriman's gravest source of concern was if indeed the Soviets were "forced" to take a unilateral approach in solving the Polish conundrum how would the American public then react.'[6]

This conception of Harriman's certainly corresponded to the agreement that Churchill and Roosevelt had made with Stalin over the division of Europe. Poland was, as has been said, an important point on which the war turned, and during the course of it was to become, in Harriman's own words, 'the touchstone of Soviet behaviour in the post-war world, the first test of Stalin's attitude toward his less powerful neighbours'.[7] In his conversations with Stalin and Molotov on 3 March 1944 Harriman emphasized that although one wished to bring about a democratic government in Poland: 'We must not let the Polish question harm relations between the two countries [America and Russia]'.[8]

Stalin, however, stuck by his refusal to recognize the exiled Polish Government and gathered together a group of Polish Communist activists in Moscow. This was to be the alternative to the exiled government in London. In the meantime the Red Army had penetrated deep into Poland, and when Harriman saw the direction that things were going he made a trip to London in May 1944. Among those he talked to was the United States ambassador to London, John G. Winant, who in all probability took a different view of the Kremlin. It was perhaps because of this that Harriman presented his views very directly and with a surprising lack of reservation. For those views directly contradicted his own government's public position. 'I explained to him the Soviet position on the question of recognition of the Polish Government in London,' Harriman wrote in a notebook. 'He had no constructive suggestions. I told him I thought our policy now should be to watch developments, *but at the appropriate time attempt to find a solution which would give the Soviet Government a completely free hand in the setting up of a government in Poland.'*[9]

A few days later, during a sitting of a 'Policy Committee' at the State Department in Washington, Harriman expressed himself in a similar manner on the Polish question. This time, however, he indicated his desired solution for the *whole* of eastern Europe: 'Our policy should be to stand on the sidelines,' he said, and in any event 'the pattern worked out between Beneš and the Soviets is the best we can expect in eastern Europe'. When queried as to how far west the 'Beneš arrangement' (that is, the 'soft Communist' option) might stretch, Harriman answered that it would certainly be applied to the Soviet Union's neighbours and in the Balkans.[10]

*

When one reads today of the decisions that were taken in this short period of time (between the end of 1943 and the capitulation of the Polish underground army on 2 October 1944) in Washington, London and Moscow one can get some idea of the enormous influence that the individuals concerned had on the fate of the future eastern bloc countries. It was probably not just chance that in all the important decisions and conferences Averell Harriman, whose background we considered in Chapter 1, played the central role as the mediator who was better informed than all the others. For Harriman belonged to those circles who cultivate the will and the power to ensure that just at the decisive historical moments (he took over the post of ambassador to Moscow just at the end of 1943) the right people are in the right places.

As we are speaking of the exploitation of crucial moments in history, it is worth mentioning another interesting example. On the return journey from Washington to Moscow at the end of May 1944 Harriman had an important conversation with the exiled Czech president Benes̆ in London. On 29 May he sent a telegram to Roosevelt, in which he reported on the contents and significance of this conversation. According to Benes̆'s information the Poles in London had secretly been in contact with the Soviet delegation in England. The exiled Polish Government had at last made the right decision, according to Harriman, and was now nearer to Moscow's position.[11] But it is extremely questionable whether Benes̆ actually conveyed this information, Larsh says at the end of his research. For the contact between the exiled Poles and the Russians was in reality merely a first attempt at a conversation and was conducted by go-betweens. What is more important to note is that this was not an initiative by the head of the exiled Polish Government, Stanlislav Mikolajczyk, as Harriman wrote, but by the Russians who, following their own interests, had undertaken this action primarily to demonstrate to the Allies their 'friendly relations with their neighbours'.

Nevertheless, the telegram of 29 May 1944 had decisive consequences for the Poles. The head of the government, Mikolajczyk, travelled to America at the beginning of June hoping to win American support at the last moment against the Bolshevik occupation of Warsaw. He was received with full honours by Roosevelt, but despite all the lofty rhetoric about the goodwill of the West, he left the White House empty-handed. For Roosevelt believed in the contents of Harriman's telegram, as his answer of 30 June makes clear.[12] He was convinced that Poland was at last going to form an alliance with the Soviet Union.

*

A month later it was all over. With fire and smoke 'Warsaw, the capital, the head, the intelligence of the erstwhile 16–17 million Poles has been extinguished,' wrote Himmler. The Poles were not prepared to hand over their country to the Bolsheviks and had therefore to revolt against the Germans when the time seemed right.

There were, of course, also deeper historical reasons for this. For centuries the culture of Poland had, in a positive sense, been influenced from all sides. Even during the Enlightenment of the eighteenth and nineteenth centuries she did not fall behind the development of the rest of Europe. Already at the time of the Reformation many Poles (above all in the sixteenth century) had turned to the Lutheran and Calvinist Churches. This brought about a lively spiritual movement that maintained itself in the many published volumes that appeared in Polish at that time. The widespread religious tolerance in the country at that time made it a haven for oppressed Protestants as well as for the Bohemian and Moravian brothers who were forming new settlements everywhere in Poland. This culture of openness and spiritual broadmindedness was, however, soon destroyed. When Stephen Bathory, a fanatical Catholic and admirer of the Society of Jesus, came to the throne in 1575, Poland was a country with a particularly strong tradition of religious freedom. He and his successor Sigismund III Vasa (who ruled from 1587 to 1632), son of the Swedish king John III who had embraced Catholicism, set the Society of Jesus on its triumphal progress in this part of Europe. A whole network of Jesuit schools and academies laid a firm foundation in Poland for the offensive of the Counter-Reformation in the whole of central and eastern Europe. Within a very short space of time Poland of all countries had become the bulwark of militant Catholicism.

Roughly two hundred years later, at the time of Lessing and Goethe, another stream of religious tolerance appeared in Poland. This strove for the ideals of the French Revolution, although without causing the kind of bloodbath seen in France. The Polish constitution of 3 May 1791, which

was later known as the Polish Testament, was a ripe fruit of
this movement of renewal. The first written constitution in
Europe, it improved the position of farmers and citizens,
envisaged free elections and was celebrated for 150 years in
Poland as a national holiday. The celebrations were termi-
nated only by the Bolshevik occupation. During these 150
years the Polish people had yet to experience many wars and
catastrophes. None of these, though, were as successful as
Bolshevism in knocking out (on the surface at any rate) the
spiritual culture of Poland, which during the course of
the nineteenth century was able to produce such truly
central European philosophers as Trentowski, Libelt and
Cieszkowski.[13]

Under the Communist regime, and through the imprison-
ing effect of the Cold War, the spiritual voice of Poland was
almost totally excluded from the development of the cultural orchestra of central Europe. It was not for nothing that
the military alliance of the Soviet bloc was cemented in
Warsaw and named the 'Warsaw Pact'. Poland was and is
the largest and most populated country in eastern central
Europe. (The Ukraine, apart from its western region, belongs wholly to eastern Europe and is considered by the
Russians to belong to the culture of the East Slavs.) The
Bolsheviks always took this fact into account and constantly
sought to answer the 'Polish question' with a firm 'yes'
to a Poland oriented towards the Soviet Union. They never
tired in their efforts to suppress the Polish people's desire
for freedom.

Here, however, they had to reckon with an important
factor which they could neither ignore nor remove from
Poland. This was the Catholic Church. Nevertheless, after
initial conflicts, the Bolsheviks soon managed to get a hold
on this force as well. They knew how to use the fact that the
Polish clergy, as Rudolf Steiner once said, 'think, feel and
sense everything through and through as true Polish nationals'.[14] For through the more lenient treatment of the Catholic

Church that it adopted after 'the demonstration of the believers' (in which over a million gathered in Czestochowa) on 25 August 1956, the Kremlin and its representatives in Warsaw were able to lull the restless Poles to sleep for a relatively long time. As long as the Church was able to re-establish itself in peace within the Communist system there reigned a kind of 'Holy Peace' (or at least a kind of peace that could be still controlled), not just in Poland but in all the countries of the Warsaw Pact. Poland, and the Polish Church in particular, was in a certain respect the key to the continued stability of the Bolshevik empire.

The Holy Solidarity with the 'New Romans'

As the young American patriot Bill Clinton entered the Loyola Hall of Georgetown University with his mother, the Jesuit priest was already waiting for them. It was autumn 1964, 20 long years before full diplomatic relations were established between the United States and the Vatican, and yet it was precisely with the aggressive representative of the Holy See that the young Baptist wished to study foreign policy. Since his meeting with John F. Kennedy, Clinton had been dreaming of his great task in life: to fight for America as a politician. He had asked several teachers and relatives about the best place in the United States to study foreign policy in order to be in a good position for a career as a diplomat. Everyone had answered: Georgetown University.[15] He later explained that he wished to study at the place with the highest academic standards for he was certain that in the coming decades America would be more and more involved in world events.[16]

After the walk through the rooms of the university, the Jesuit wished to find out whether or not the newcomer fitted into the milieu of Georgetown University. 'What foreign language do you know?' he asked. 'None, sir,' was the

answer. The Jesuit was shocked: 'What in the name of the
Holy Father is a Southern Baptist who can't speak a foreign
language doing in the *mother* of all Jesuit schools?!' he asked.
When they were outside, Clinton said to his mother, 'Don't
you worry, mother. They will know what I'm doing here
when I've been here a while.'[17]

The young Clinton had a right to be this self-confident.
For the Jesuits always look out for just those people who are
prepared to exercise unlimited amounts of will-power to
achieve particular goals. Clinton was and is just such a
person. It was because of this that the atmosphere in the
'mother of all Jesuit schools' was so appealing. There he was
not only strongly influenced by Professor Carroll Quigley[18]
but also by the Jesuit teachers who came from 'all over the
world' in order to instruct the future presidents and diplomats of the United States in the secrets of international world
politics. It was above all the Hungarian Father Joseph Sebes,
who had been a missionary in China almost all his life and
who now taught as the Dean of the faculty for international
diplomacy, who impressed Clinton most with his course on
world religions and their role in history.[19]

*

It is not only in Washington that the endeavours of Catholic
orders go hand in hand with the intentions of influential
western circles. As a matter of fact there are many examples
for that. One can cite the very fruitful co-operation between
the Vatican Bank ('God's own bank'), the CIA and various
Masonic lodges (above all the 'Propaganda 2', P2) which in
Italy are always coming to light following scandals and
cases of corruption. (That which comes to the surface in Italy
as a result of revelations and crimes remains hidden in other
countries. This does not mean, though, that these forces are
any less active in those countries!) In 1978 Mino Pecorelli,
journalist and editor of an information sheet at the OP News

Agency, published a list of more than a hundred Masonic lodge brethren from the Vatican. An indication of just how near his list came to the truth was given six months later when he was murdered, on 20 March 1978. Mino Pecorelli was a genuine insider, a member of the P2 lodge (he wrote other reports on the P2 lodge and its relationship to the Vatican), and as such his punishment for betrayal had to be particularly harsh.[20]

Whenever it is a question of developing their long-term plans, which always take into account spiritual impulses and the laws of history, these two fundamentally antagonistic groups will often come together. Rudolf Steiner spoke a number of times about the fact that at the global level, since the end of the eighteenth century, the higher echelons of Freemasonry have been infiltrated by Jesuits. By appearing to keep the external enmity between the two 'secret forces' well stoked up, however, the uninitiated members of such orders can be kept in a state of confusion, 'for that is something which in this area belongs to politics, to a real steering of human beings' said Steiner.[21] A consequence of this strategy has been that the whole public life of Europe and the West has, indirectly, become more and more spiritually confused during recent centuries, so that today people are very easily influenced.

*

The Cold War of the 60s and 70s was only frosty in an outward sense. Inwardly, humanity was, since the 60s, heading towards an important historical transformation, which Rudolf Steiner described as being decisive for the further development or, alternatively, to the downfall of humanity. This was, of course, known by the occultists of the Vatican as well as the West. It was also known at what time this transformation would dramatically break through to the surface, among other things in the form of powerful impulses for freedom in central and eastern Europe. The outbreak and the strength of these timely revolutions cannot be prevented, they thought in these circles, but we must do everything in our power to ensure that we can use the results of these outbreaks for *our own ends.*

The first preparations for this great undertaking began in the 70s. In Poland the attempts of the new head of the party and government, Eduard Gierek, to bring forward the pace of industrialization in his backward country by taking out foreign loans was given full support by the West in the form of billions of dollars credit. But it was only in 1978 that one could perceive the actual start of the operation: a signal was consciously sent forth from Rome with the election of the first non-Italian Pope since 1523. The Catholic Church was preparing for a new phase in its attempts to influence world affairs. The starting-point of this enterprise was to be eastern Europe—above all Poland—hence the election of the Polish Cardinal Archbishop of Cracow, Karol Wojtyla. This was of enormous significance for the political situation in eastern Europe, a fact that was probably not fully perceived by all participants at the elections. Most of the cardinals who took part in the conclave (the gathering at which the cardinals elect a new Pope) had, as non-Europeans, little notion of the political and strategic significance of Poland.[22]

In Poland as well as in certain ecclesiastical centres in Europe (especially in France, the bastion of Catholicism in the West, where Poland is always regarded with a special interest) it was understood very well what the Vatican's signal meant. A few months after the election there appeared in the French periodical *Esprit* an article by Tadeusz Mazowiecki—then vice-president of the legally recognized Catholic Intelligence Club and by 1989 the first post-war non-Communist Polish prime minister—in which the significance of the Vatican move for the Catholic intelligentsia of France and for the Catholics of Poland (95 per cent of the population) was described in the following way:

'Immediately after the election of Pope John Paul II, I received a letter from Paul Thibaud, the editor-in-chief of the French monthly *Esprit*, which included the, for Polish ears, very pleasant observation that this election was an act that was both reconciliatory and proper . . . Here someone was speaking to us from abroad in a way which understood our Polish feelings . . . The Poles—*and certainly not only they*— saw in this election the courageous breaking of the 450-year-old tradition of electing only Italians to the Papacy . . . and also (they looked upon it) with great satisfaction, or, better said, as a long-awaited moral compensation for Poland and for the whole Second Communist world.'[23] Catholic circles *on both sides of the Iron Curtain* then experienced this deed with political ramifications on a *global scale*.

Eduard Gierek, the head of the Polish Communist party in Warsaw, sent warm patriotic words of greeting to the first Polish Pope. The Pope did not wait for long and by early 1979 had written his first Encyclical in which he spoke of human rights that were to be applied without any regard to differences of entitlement. The Holy See linked this to a concrete strategy for the future of the Pope's homeland. That the Polish government immediately sanctioned the so-called pilgrimage of the Pope who was preaching the 'theology of liberation from Bolshevism' was in large measure thanks to the softening up effect of the huge credits extended by the West. The Bolshevists were apparently not in a position to see what was about to happen to them.

On 5 June 1979, a Vatican plane landed for the first time at Warsaw airport. Out of it stepped 'the flying Pope' accompanied by several western television camera teams. In a series of sermons to huge, ecstatic crowds (some six million in all) his trip opened up a new phase of religious-national awakening in Poland. 'Every person and every people needs hope,' wrote Tadeusz Mazowiecki in April 1981 of this 'historic hour' in the leading article in the first edition of the weekly newspaper of Solidarity:

Pope John Paul II (above).

In June 1983 over one million people gathered in
Warsaw Stadium to welcome the Pope on his second visit
to his homeland.

. . . Without hope no one can live. In history, however, there are seldom moments when something appears before us that is the expression of hope for a whole people. Such a moment we experienced for the first time in June 1979 during the course of the nine days of the first papal visit to Poland. When John Paul II prayed at Victory Square in Warsaw in the words of the Psalmist: 'May Thy Spirit descend and change the face of the earth, *this earth*' [emphasis in original], we suddenly felt that he spoke those words about us and for us. We knew that they expressed our common longing for hope, and we felt the power in those words. *This was not only a religious but a social and national event of great, incomparable significance.* It had its effect on everyone's attitude and represented a call to society to organize itself . . . The Pope showed us a way in which we could fight for our rights without hatred . . . and made us aware of the great power which lies in human dignity [author's italics].[24]

Some months after this visit by the Pope its effects were discernible in the form of a political earthquake. When in the summer of 1980 a concrete pretext for action was found—namely, a sharp rise in prices and inflation due to commodity shortages—nationwide strikes followed. After months of hesitation, the government was forced to begin talks at the Lenin shipyard in Gdansk. After endless night-long sessions it was agreed on 31 August to permit the existence of the first non-Communist trade union (Solidarity). A considerable number of other concessions were made by the government. Despite this the conflict continued to assume dangerous proportions for Poland's national sovereignty—severely restricted as it then was— at least five times over the next few months. The ongoing economic misery as well as the rivalries within the ten million members of Solidarity made the situation ever more tense. The expectations of the repressed population were too great to maintain the tactical restraint that the Pope had demanded during his private audience with Lech Walesa in January 1981 at the Vatican. For if everything had gone according to plan it would not have developed into a full-blown crisis by the end of 1981. In November the Holy See announced a second pastoral visit to Poland, but the tensions in Wojtyla's homeland had already become too great.

The Kremlin was from the outset not at all happy with the apparent compliance of the Polish Government with the 'Catholic rebellion' and planned to march 18 'friendly' divisions into Poland in December 1980. This time, however, American president Jimmy Carter reacted unusually decisively and quickly against the build-up of Warsaw Pact troops along the Polish border. Over the hotline to Moscow he warned Soviet party leader Brezhnev on 3 December of the political and economic consequences that would follow Soviet military intervention: no wheat for the Soviet Union, no exports of technology, further arming of NATO, and military co-operation (of the US) with China and Japan. So there was little left for the Kremlin to do but to dictate an 'internal solution'. In Poland martial law was declared on 12 December 1981 on account of the increasing weakness of the whole Polish economy and due to the pressure being exerted upon General W. Jaruzelski by the Kremlin.

*

An unusual meeting was held in the Vatican Library on 7 June 1982. What took place then between Ronald Reagan and the Pope during their 50 minutes of discussion was first made public ten years later in a 'special report' for *Time* magazine. The extraordinarily interesting report by Carl Bernstein[25] sought to create the impression that the eastern European strategy of the United States and the Vatican in the 1980s was the result of an idealistic initiative taken by these two leaders. But in fact the detailed information given by Bernstein betrays the real nature of this strategy, which always reckons with long-term developments in history. In the report an American diplomat familiar with the details of the plot to keep Solidarity alive is quoted as saying, 'The Washington-Vatican alliance "didn't cause the fall of Communism. Like all great and lucky leaders, *the Pope and the President exploited the forces of history to their own ends*".'[26]

'The campaign by Washington and the Vatican to keep Solidarity alive began immediately after General Wojciech Jaruzelski declared martial law,' reported Bernstein. 'Shortly after . . . Reagan called the Pope for his advice.' His Holiness had, however, already reacted to the new situation in his homeland. According to the American secret service, reported *Time*, the Pope had already recommended to Walesa through Church channels that Solidarity go underground and remain active there. In addition, all ten million members must be directed not to take to the streets because of the danger of a direct confrontation with the military, which could well escalate into civil war. On one of the following days the American secretary of state Alexander Haig, an enthusiastic member of the Church, sent a special ambassador to see the Pope. At that time Washington and the Vatican still did not have full diplomatic relations. Despite this, the 'ambassador at large', Vernon Walters, himself a devout Catholic, was received with full honours and held long conversations with the Pope as well as with his secretary of state Cardinal Casaroli. The agreement drawn up shortly afterwards between Reagan and Pope John Paul II for the execution of a '*clandestine campaign* to hasten the break-up of the Communist empire' was declared, by another Catholic in the Reagan Cabinet, national security advisor Richard Allen, to be 'one of the great secret alliances of all time'.[27] We might recall here that in 1982 there was no word anywhere in the media of the imminent demise of Communism. How then could Reagan and the Pope speak of a 'hastening' of this unknown break-up? To this question there is no answer even in Bernstein's 'Special Report'.

A large-scale programme then got underway. Many tons of communications equipment, computers, video cameras and photocopiers were smuggled into Poland through various channels between 1982 and 1989. As Zbigniew Brzezinski,[28] former advisor to President Carter, said: 'This wasn't about spending huge amounts of money. It was about getting the message out and resisting: books, communications equipment, propaganda, ink and printing presses.'[29]

Even if, according to Brzezinski, billions were not involved, surely many millions must have been provided for 'Operation Solidarity'. Bernstein and other sources have stated that the money came from the CIA, from American funds and from the notorious Vatican Bank. American agents and Catholic priests worked closely together in the enterprise. Vatican agents in Poland were the most important channels between Solidarity activists and Rome-Washington. 'The Vatican's information was absolutely better and quicker than ours in every respect,' said Alexander Haig.[30] This was hardly surprising considering that for every US agent in Poland the Pope would have had many thousands of potential helpers on hand!

The key to the success of the operation lay in the linking of American patriotism with devout Catholics in Washington. All the main actors in Washington were supporters of the Holy See: CIA chief William Casey, Richard Allen (Reagan's first national security advisor), William Clark (Allen's successor), Alexander Haig, Vernon Walters (personal go-between between John Paul II and Reagan, ambassador at large and former CIA officer) and William Wilson. When the United States and the Vatican established full diplomatic relations on 10 January 1984, Reagan naturally nominated the devout William Wilson as his first ambassador to the Holy City; a common language with his colleagues at the Vatican was of course necessary. These people had after all a direct effect on events in Poland: 'On almost all his trips to Europe and the Middle East [CIA chief] Casey flew first to Rome, so that he could meet with John Paul II and exchange information,' writes Bernstein.[31] 'Our information about Poland was very well founded because the bishops were in continual contact with the Holy See and Solidarity,' explains Cardinal Silvestrini, the Vatican's deputy secretary of state at that time. 'They informed us about prisoners, about the activities and needs of Solidarity groups and about the attitude and schisms in the government. All this information was communicated to the President or Casey.'[3]

*

Exactly seven years before the fall of the Berlin Wall the Vatican organized a 'Europe festival' in Santiago de Compostela in Spain. The Polish Pope John Paul II spoke out clearly to thousands of enthusiastic supporters on 9 November 1982:

Despite the bloody conflicts that have raged between the peoples of Europe and despite the spiritual crises that have rocked this continent . . . after two thousand years of its history one must concede that a European identity without Christianity is unimaginable, and that in Christianity we find those common roots out of which the civilization of this continent has grown: its culture, its dynamism, its enterprise, its capacity to spread itself to other continents, in short, all that it is renowned for . . . *When Europe is unified* which, with all due consideration to the differences within European culture, including political systems, she can one day be . . . then her future will no longer be ruled by fear and uncertainty, but will be one in which she will, both inwardly and outwardly, open up a new era of life which will be a blessing for the whole world.[33]

If such a sentence had been spoken by an idealistic philosophical thinker one could hardly find fault with it. But what matters here is who is speaking! And when Pope John Paul II, protector and promoter of militant Catholicism in the form of *Opus Dei*, speaks of Christianity there can be no doubt that he means the Catholic Church. Seven years after his speech, the continent of Europe, now freed from Bolshevism, *must*, according to his ideal, now overcome its cultural and political differences by returning to a 'common hierarchy of values'.[34] By this is, of course, meant the dogmas ('values') and 'hierarchies' of the Holy Father.

For those who might ask how Europe would look in concrete terms were it to be 're-Catholicized', some interesting pointers have indeed emerged from time to time. If one disregards the moralizing rhetoric which often accompanies them, such pointers indicate a clear concept of the further expansion of the European Union (EU). In May 1994 Zbigniew Brzezinski, one of the connoisseurs of international politics, the son of a Polish diplomat and today a professor at John Hopkins University in the USA, sketched out the future of Europe in the following way:

The best design would be an enlarged European Union embracing the European Free Trade Area countries [today that can only mean Switzerland] and eventually also reaching into central Europe to include at least three Visegrad nations: the Czech Republic, Hungary and Poland. These three nations should be enrolled by NATO as well.

A Europe along these lines would envelop Germany while enhancing the German role within it. Attaining this goal will require continued exercise of political leadership by France and Germany. Beyond that, it will call for profound and genuine—not just formal—German-Polish reconciliation matching the existing German-French reconciliation.

A French-German-Polish coalition would provide a mighty inner core for a larger Europe. It would further affirm an historically positive role for an economically powerful, politically constructive and truly European Germany. Such a trilateral strategic coalition—incorporating 175 million citizens (more than Russia!)—would be economically driven by Germany that was politically balanced by France and Poland. It would expand the scope of Europe and enhance security on the whole continent.[35]

This vision of the future has already in its external form today—at the end of 1994—become a tangible reality. Brzezinski describes it simply in terms of strategy, while others sharing his vision portray it in a more idealistic or religious form. But Brzezinski is by no means the only one who has sketched out this development in such clear terms. In the British periodical *International Affairs*, for example, there appeared (in July 1994) an article that dealt in a very detailed and thorough manner with the eastward expansion of the EU. At the end the author, a lecturer at the University of Essex, came to exactly the same conclusion as Brzezinski and described a future 'Paris-Berlin-Warsaw axis'.[36]

The spiritual content of this 'New Holy Alliance' is even more evident than the form of its actualization. France, *the* bastion of Catholicism in Western Europe, has already been trying for decades, with the full backing of Germany, to inject into the EU the spirit of the Vatican. This can be seen in the tireless advocacy of the politics of centralization promoted by the Catholic Jacques Delors and in the 'Holy Friendship' between François Mitterand and Helmut Kohl.

How is it, though, that the Germans have once again become 'hitched' to the spirit of Rome? Those seeking an answer to this should recall a meeting that took place in 1958

THE 'NEW HOLY ALLIANCE'

outside Paris. It was there that the freshly inaugurated President General de Gaulle presented his visitor Konrad Adenauer with the 'marriage' contract. 'Three things,' he pontificated, 'were being asked for from France by the defeated Germany. First was support for Germany's efforts to regain the respect and trust of other countries; second was a guarantee of security in the face of the Soviet threat; third was the recognition of Germany's right to reunification.' And the price? Bonn must support Paris's agricultural policies within the Common Market and France's eternal battles with the English, but above all Germany must help France to fulfil her *'mission in the world', her role as a great power.*[37] Adenauer was certainly aware that France's 'mission' has for centuries been intimately bound up with the 'mission' of the Papacy. Helping France to resurrect her 'old glory' meant for Germany co-operation with Romanism; this element manifests itself on a political level through France's role as a great power.

If this connection between Paris and Warsaw via Berlin were really to be established then the whole of Europe could serve as a bulwark of the spirit of Rome. The servants of this spirit had always regarded the renewal of the power that Rome had in the Middle Ages as their highest ideal. The creation of such an axis would, however, also be greeted with great enthusiasm by the occult circles of the West. For this would, at least for a while, practically destroy the potential of cultural collaboration between central Europe and the eastern Slavs. And what would become of the cultural task of central Europe, which was discussed in earlier chapters and in the Foreword of this book? Brzezinski envisages the task of Germany as being the economic motor for Europe. No cultural let alone spiritual role is foreseen here. Germany is evidently intended to lend further support to France's 'mission in the world' (soldiers of this 'former' world power are today active in 33 countries!).[38] In Poland, which actually also belongs to central Europe, it is highly likely that the clergy will become directly or indirectly even more powerful.

*

Do the plans for erecting a 'New Holy Alliance' correspond to the wishes of the people in the envisaged axis countries? One can say with certainty that this is not the case. These intentions merely express the will of some groups who have for several centuries been concerning themselves with the deeper spiritual impulses of world history and who ceaselessly attempt to use those impulses in the service of their own *spiritual* power.

Such circles, which cling to ancient occult traditions, have in recent centuries had to concern themselves with a fundamentally new problem. This arises more and more frequently in the form of the *individuality that wills to awaken*. Despite all obstacles and diversions there also, from time to time, appear personalities on the political stage who bear this quality, at least in seed form. If such personalities were supported, both directly and indirectly, by cultivating 'a culture of wakefulness' in various spheres of life, then it would not be possible for the circles mentioned above to achieve their *actual* goals. For in the final analysis, their aim is to exercise a covert influence on the cultural-spiritual evolution of humanity, and the prerequisite for the long-term success of their efforts is the maintaining of this camouflage.

The ceaseless struggle to develop a culture in which independent judgement of social and political events becomes a habit of life can therefore be of real use to thwart these plans. In this sense everyone can make his or her own contribution in opposing the cultural decline which the New Holy Alliance is destined to bring about.

oppose political correctness?

8
The Changing Face of Europe: Part Two

The Beginning of a 'New Holy Alliance'

Soon after the fall of the Berlin Wall in November 1989, many people realized that 'the end of the Cold War had brought the European Community's moment of truth much closer'.[1] But it was still some time before the celebrations of the fiftieth anniversary of the Allied landings in Normandy (6 June 1944) and the perhaps not accidentally almost simultaneous departure of the wartime Allies' forces from Berlin brought the theme to light once again. In an article at the beginning of May 1994, which has already been discussed in the previous chapter, the Polish expert on global strategy, Zbigniew Brzezinski, considered this issue and came to the questionable conclusion that the political, not merely economic, expansion of the European Union in all directions, and especially to the east, was both unavoidable and desirable. The welfare of an enlarged Europe, he wrote, would be dependent on the establishment of a strategic 'Franco-German-Polish coalition'. Such a 'mighty inner core' would 'expand the scope of Europe and would enhance the security of the whole continent.'[2]

*

At the beginning of July 1994, a month after the Normandy celebrations, Bill Clinton visited Berlin. It was the first time that the visit of an American president had not had to concern itself with the security of NATO's western frontier. Here, in the city of the former defeated enemy, he stayed

overnight—again, the first American president to do so—
and sought repeatedly in speeches and gestures to under-
line the fact that the former victors felt themselves today to
be the closest allies of a Germany which was united and
embedded in Europe.

But the most significant dimension of the visit lay not, as
was reported by the media, in harking back to the memories
of the difficult times of the blockade of West Berlin and the
speech of J.F. Kennedy, which had given courage to the
inhabitants of the beleaguered city and had supported them
with promises of help from the West. Rather, it was the
conference between Bill Clinton, Helmut Kohl, and Jacques
Delors on 12 July at the Reichstag, and hardly noticed by the
media, which was the most significant and expressive symptom of what was to come in Europe.

A month later Stuart E. Eizenstat, the US ambassador to
the EU, stated that President Clinton had taken this opportunity 'to give the clearest expression of unequivocal support for the historic process of European integration *that a
US president had ever given*. He emphasized that he felt a
commitment not only to the welfare of the EU as presently
constituted, but also saw a stronger, more fully responsible
and more autonomous Europe as a positive power for
America.'[3]

Helmut Kohl did not take part in this conference as the
representative of Germany, but as presiding EU president.
(Shortly before, on 1 July 1994, Germany had assumed the
six-monthly EU presidency.) The meeting of the highest
representatives of the European Union (Delors and Kohl)
with the representative of the former protector of western
Europe, just on the day when American forces departed
from Berlin, had—albeit unnoticed by the public—the character of a ceremonial transfer of power.

*

Observation of world events in the second half of 1994 leads to the conclusion that one can hardly ignore the way in which they inwardly relate to some important symptoms characterized by Rudolf Steiner in one of his lectures given during the last days of the First World War. In this lecture Steiner characterized England and France as the bearers of the national element in the modern era. 'France,' he said, 'modifies the national element within the national state in such a way that the national element tends to *transform the inner being of man* . . . In England the *personal element* transcends nationalism and seeks to embrace the *whole world* . . . This phenomenon, strangely enough, manifests itself also geographically, especially when we consider . . . the turning-point at which Napoleon, who was born out of the Revolution, lost the Battle of Trafalgar to the English in 1805. What reveals itself to us here? Napoleon, certainly a unique figure, and yet still a true representative of the French spirit, signifies the turning inwards, geographically also, the turning inwards to the continent of Europe . . . as a consequence of the Battle of Trafalgar, Napoleon is thrust back towards Europe, while England is thrust outwards to the whole world . . . Looking back a few decades before this date we see in North America how Romanism, that nuance which has worked within French culture, was forced back on a world scale by the Anglo-Saxon element.'[4] (In 1763, after the end of the Seven Years' War, England acquired almost all the French colonies in North America.)

After the end of the Cold War in 1989—exactly 72 years after the Anglo-Saxon element, this time represented by the power of the USA, returned to the continent of Europe—one can see a certain metamorphosed repetition of the process described above. For when the last US soldiers pulled down their flags and left Berlin on 8 September 1994, the 50-year *Pax Americana* ended for western Europe. Now it was no longer a question of 'the emancipation of the personality within the national element', which Rudolf Steiner described in the lecture referred to above as being in a sense a legitimate impulse for that time. Today, it is much more a question of the economic power of America and its allies in the Anglo-Saxon world wishing to concentrate on the great 'world war' of the coming epoch—the great *economic* world war (at the root of which, of course, lie spiritual conflicts). Further, the 'most important' goal of Washington after the collapse of the Soviet Union has become 'the shaping of co-operative relations' with Russia. Another power is now required to take on the leadership of western and central Europe. And this could only be achieved through 'the progressive deepening of the political union of Europe and the extension of its security sphere'.[5]

How disinclined the Americans are today to play their previous role as the leading military and political power in Europe is evident from their behaviour with regard to the war in the Balkans. Again and again they have made it clear that not a single American soldier will be sent there, and they kept to it as long as the war was going on. The fact that their allies, the British, had troops stationed there essentially signifies that the Anglo-Saxon world is not pre-pared to hand over the EU completely to the French, the 'representatives of Romanism'. For the USA, a strong British presence in the European Union is economically indis-pensable. This became clear a year ago, for example, when the eighth round of GATT negotiations were successfully concluded despite great difficulties thanks to the natural co-operation of the British Trade Commissioner Sir Leon Britten (EU) and the Americans.

'Three Countries at the Heart of the Continent . . .'

The preparations for the EC's coming 'moment of truth', in which the Roman element would experience the renewal of its position of power in the continent over which it had once reigned supreme, was described in the previous chapter. But how far has the Franco-German-Polish axis, which I characterized there as the New Holy Alliance, already become reality?

Already on 28 August 1991, shortly after Germany recognized the western frontier of Poland for the first time, the foreign ministers of France, Germany and Poland met in Weimar. The European public at the time was concerned with the highly emotional topic of the struggles around the besieged coastal cities of Croatia. The conditions were thus just right for the first official ministerial conference of the future alliance members to pass completely unnoticed. In their common declaration, the three ministers—having not without reason chosen to meet on the birthday and in the city of Goethe—pointed in clear language to the significance of this decisive moment for the future of Europe: 'Europe stands at a momentous crossroads in its history,' began the declaration:

> Its peoples and states have begun to walk the path to new forms of living together. We are aware that *Poles, Germans and Frenchmen* bear a crucial responsibility for the achievement of viable structures of European neighbourliness.
>
> We now have *a single chance* to develop the new Europe in a spirit of common responsibility and of human solidarity . . . and upon the *inherited foundation of common values* [the 'common values' recall in the first instance, at least as far as France and Poland are concerned, the Roman Catholic tradition] . . . The strength of the new Europe lies in the manifold vitality of its institutions. The European Community *is its kernel*. It must carry forward its integration . . .

'Today, on Goethe's birthday,' the foreign ministers of the future coalition explained, in conclusion, that they had decided 'to meet once a year from now on—or whenever the situation in Europe requires it—also to hold irregular sessions.'

Scarcely eight months had passed before the next gathering of the three ministers at Bergerac in France on 24 April
1992. The Treaty of Maastricht had been concluded in the
meantime in December 1991. Perhaps because of this one
could conceive that the three allies already had a much
clearer, more concrete picture of their future co-operation:
'The common aim of Poland, Germany and France,' went their
official declaration, *'is the establishment of a free and united
Europe . . .* [italics in original] *'.*

New dangers have emerged. The reawakening of exaggerated nationalisms as well as . . . economic difficulties
involve social tensions. These challenges can only be
met by a real partnership across our entire continent . . .
On the occasion of its extraordinary conference with
foreign and defence ministers of central, eastern, and
southern Europe, the Western European Union will press
for far-reaching co-operation on these issues. *Poland, Germany and France intend to play a dynamic role in the area
covered in these institutionalized dialogues.*
Germany, France and Poland pursue the aim of the
creation of a common economic space in Europe . . . We
welcome the signing of the European Treaty between the
European Community and Poland . . . The European
Treaty opens up for Poland greater commercial possibilities and will facilitate the extension and diversification of
technical assistance programmes. France and Germany
will commit themselves to concretizing the perspectives
for accession [to the Treaty of Rome] which this Treaty
opens up for Poland.

The members of the future 'European axis' also expressed
their common position with respect to the war in southern
Europe. But this 'commonality' was strongly informed
by the very traditional 'special interests' that have been
behind the French involvement in the Balkan conflict:
'Naturally we condemn the violence, which has further

spread in Bosnia-Hercegovina through armed groups with the support of regular armed forces, notably the Yugoslav federal army. We call on all parties to hold firmly to the terms of the agreed cease-fire.' At this meeting the three foreign ministers spent considerable time discussing the wars in the Caucasus (around Karabakh) and in Afghanistan, in other words, matters outside the continent of Europe. They expressed their common position on these subjects in a separate communiqué.

At the next summit of the foreign ministers of the 'New Holy Alliance', on 11 and 12 November 1993 in Warsaw, the results of their co-operation had become more visible. In their final declaration the question of Poland's rapid entry into the EU was a central theme: 'We affirm that Poland and the other associated nations in central and eastern Europe are eligible to join the European Union ... In view of the fact that co-operation with the associated nations is directed towards the goal of entry *Germany and France will extend every assistance to Poland in this process* [author's italics].'

The three had spoken quite concretely about various areas of co-operation. Two years previously, for example, moves for the establishment of the Europacorps (the 'United Armed Forces of Europe') were initiated by Mitterand and Kohl. Scarcely had the first Franco-German unit been assembled when the German and French foreign ministers took note of Poland's desire *'to establish contacts between the Europacorps and the Polish armed forces'*.

Finally, the ministers mentioned a few more concrete actions including:

... provisions for regular consultations between the three foreign ministers; the continuation of interparliamentary contacts which began with the meeting between the Foreign Affairs Committees of the parliaments of our countries in November 1992 in Bonn; the bringing together of the Institut Français, the Goethe Institut and a

Polish Institute in one building in Warsaw with the aim of fostering intimate cooperation in common activities in the cultural realm; close co-operation between the Franco-German Youth League with the German-Polish League for the realization of trilateral youth movements.

We wish to encourage German, French and Polish regional and municipal authorities, universities, schools and other cultural organizations to follow the example of our co-operation.

In his concluding speech to all this (in awarding the German-Polish Prize) the German foreign minister Klaus Kinkel said:

> Our threefold meeting today has reminded us that *Poland is a European heartland like France and Germany.*
>
> Mutual trust and affection have developed between Germany and France over the years. We Germans wish to enrich our relationship with Poland with a similar spirit . . .

Enlarging the 'Hard Core' of Europe

31 August 1994 was an epoch-making date for Europe. Fifty years after the first incursions of Soviet troops into the territory of the Third Reich, this day marked a significant milestone in history: the last Russian troops left Berlin and, at the same time, central Europe. For half a century western Europe had stood in the shadow of the oppressive military might of the former eastern superpower. More than 400,000 Soviet soldiers alone were stationed between the Elbe and the Oder. Now, however, five years after the fall of the Berlin Wall, the end of the Russian military presence in Berlin was treated by the public as a matter of course.

But this was at the same time a symptom of the fact that the five-year ripening phase of the new era had also ended; scarcely had *one day* gone by before there burst open, like some great earthquake in human consciousness, the great debate on the subject of the 'core of Europe'. For the public at large it seemed as if it were merely accidental that just on 1 September Chancellor Kohl's party, the CDU, published its 'Proposals for European Policy', recommendations for a 'blitz-strategy' for expansion of the EU. Yet this Europe Document from the CDU had already been waiting a year for this historic moment.

The *Europa Papier* actually contained no new ideas on the enlargement of the EU that had not previously been put forward in many places by friends of the burgeoning 'United States of Europe'. But what was little noticed was the authors' extraordinarily clear characterization of the future relations between France and Germany (described in the document as representing 'the core of the hard core of Europe'):

Franco-German relations must advance to a qualitatively higher stage, if the historical flow of the process of European integration is to achieve its political goal and not become bogged down. Therefore *no vital decisions relating to foreign or European affairs should be taken without Franco-German co-ordination* ... For Germany, its relationship to France is today even more than before the decisive gauge of its inner affiliation to the political and cultural community of values of the West ... this is all the more the case today, as the USA is no longer able to play its role in the same way since the end of the East-West conflict.[6]

That the USA now had other priorities besides the protection of western Europe was demonstrated very modestly, far from Brussels and Berlin, a day after the spectacular publication of the *Europa Papier*. On 2 September the United States and Russia began their first joint military exercises near Tuzk in the southern Urals. Two hundred and fifty soldiers from each of the former rival superpowers took part in nine days of exercises in the field, which were described, according to the latest fashion, as 'UN peacekeeping exercises'. Those first days of September thus saw simultaneous new manoeuvrings by the forces within and around Europe; the Americans were now looking to take care of their relations with Russia. In western and central Europe another power was assuming the leadership.

*

A week after the Russian army left Berlin, the western Allies, including of course the French, withdrew their own troops on 8 September. And yet it was just at that time that the Franco-Roman renaissance was making political moves in the direction of central Europe. For the analysis of the *Europa Papier* was quite realistic when it saw the barometer of Germany's orientation to the 'political and economic community of values of the West' lying in its relation to Roman Catholic France (the word 'West' takes on an unusual connotation here).

The new relationships in Europe received further ceremonial expression a few days after the withdrawal of western troops from Berlin. The first manoeuvres of 'the Partnership for Peace' between NATO and eastern European states began on 12 September 1994 at a Polish military exercise site near Poznan. Nine hundred troops from various western countries exercised together with former Warsaw Pact units for the first time since the Second World War. It was not by accident that this symbolic exercise, in which a total of 13 countries participated, took place in Poland, the model student among those countries applying for membership of NATO.

*

One day earlier, on 11 September, Pope John Paul II arrived in Zagreb. Prior to his long-awaited visit to Croatia, the Cardinal of Zagreb, Archbishop Kuharik, said that the Croatians burned with enthusiasm for the Holy See no less than the Poles. And indeed the Polish Pope was able to conduct masses in Zagreb the like of which had not been seen in recent years in Europe. Memories of events in Poland—such as in the glory days of Solidarity in the 80s—were evoked quite spontaneously. Both the Pope and President Tudjman made much of the fact that the Croats had journeyed to their present homeland more than 1,300 years ago from 'White Croatia', a region of southern Poland. President Tudjman thanked the Holy Father for having been the first head of state to recognize Croatia's independence. More than a million enthusiastic supporters of Rome took part in the celebrations.

The Heart of a New World Power

Before the historic NATO exercise mentioned above had ended in Poland, an important conference took place in a Catholic monastery in Bamberg, north of Nuremberg. Once again the three foreign ministers of France, Germany and Poland, largely unnoticed by the media, were meeting to discuss the 'trilateral role' of their nations in Europe. But now, after three years of hard work together, they were in a position to draw up a first balance sheet of their activities. 'Decisive steps have been taken during the last years on the path towards a united Europe,' declared their final communiqué.

We shall strengthen the co-operation of our three countries in the heart of the Continent in order to work together for a united Europe... We express our satisfaction that the agreement between Poland and the European Union signed on 1 February 1994 is now in force. It is now a matter of applying it dynamically ... France and Germany welcome Poland's application for membership of the EU and assure her of their support.

Poland has been the first country to enter into a partnership programme with NATO and has been hosting the first joint military manoeuvres ... Germany and France will support Poland in her efforts to get closer to NATO ... We are very pleased to acknowledge the close and promising co-operation of the Youth Leagues which have been working towards the realization of trilateral youth movements ... We shall further promote trilateral endeavours ... [We look] with satisfaction on the progress made in bringing together the Institut Français, the Goethe Institut, and the Europe Centre of the University in Warsaw ... We welcome the establishment of regular consultations between the planning staffs and other departments of the three foreign ministries and have taken note with interest of their joint proposals for the further deepening of trilateral co-operation.

With still 'greater satisfaction' the three partners noted the fact that military co-operation between their 'three nations in the heart of the Continent' had become more concrete, as was indeed the case in all other areas. After this meeting at the Bamberg monastery, the third trilateral meeting of the *defence ministers* of Germany, Poland and France had taken place on 20 October 1994. What occasioned this was the 'Concord' exercise, in which units from the three countries participated. As we have seen, the Poles had already the year before expressed 'the wish for contact between the Europacorps and the Polish armed forces'. Now, with the first joint exercise between the Europacorps and a Polish army company, such contacts had received a special première. The units of the 'United European Armed Forces' are not divided on national lines as was the case in

Germany's foreign minister Klaus Kinkel at the conference of
the three foreign ministers in the Catholic monastery
of Bamberg, Germany.

the NATO exercise in Poland six weeks before. Germans and Frenchmen were here united in the same brigade, functioning as the kernel of the 'United European Armed Forces' which have been called for from various quarters. It should come as no surprise that the first non-Franco-German force to take part in a Europacorps exercise was an entire Polish brigade, and that in this première the *French* Euro-brigade General Friedrich shared joint command with the *Polish* Colonel Kolosa. For, as the German defence minister Volkerr Rühe said at a press conference, it was necessary to attach 'a political significance to the exercise held by Polish, French and German soldiers and precisely to such a trilateralism . . . which went far beyond practical military purposes'.

*

What would be happening in Europe today if the foreign ministers of France, Germany and Poland understood the spiritual and cultural impulses of the personality on whose birthday they had held their first trilateral conference in Weimar (28 August 1991)? The question must remain an abstract one. For it is not only the foreign ministers of these three great nations who know almost nothing of Goethe's cultural impulse. Goetheanism is no more relied upon by Europeans today than it was in the time of Rudolf Steiner, who in 1918 described Goethe's impulse as 'actually completely unknown in the widest circles, and in particular unknown, totally unknown, by those university professors of the history of literature who give lectures on Goethe, Lessing, Herder and the others . . .'[7]

Behind the world-view of Goethe, who admired the ancient cultures of Rome and Greece and the medieval tradition of France, stands the spirit which—as Rudolf Steiner put it in the last weeks of the First World War—'in the truest sense of the word is the most modern spirit of the fifth post-Atlantean epoch'.[8] For not only was Goethe able to take up within himself all the great cultures of the past, he could also, as a modern human being, survey all cultures from the viewpoint of the free individuality. This is exactly the true European ideal of the fifth post-Atlantean epoch: Europe should co-operate in the sign of individualism, and never again under the domination of a particular tradition, even if it is one that bears witness to a past as great as that of the Roman Catholic Church. If the culture of the free spiritual life is not anchored as the fundamental character of the new Europe, there will be no chance of realizing either the joint economic institutions of the EU or the peaceful coexistence of the many political communities in Europe.

'Goetheanism,' said Rudolf Steiner at that time, 'is *nothing national*, Goetheanism is nothing German . . . ' for 'Goethe himself said . . . that these three personalities [Spinoza, Shakespeare and the Swedish naturalist Linné] had had the greatest influence on him . . . Goetheanism could work in all truly human thinking, could work in the religious life . . . could work in the forms of human social life, *Goetheanism could work in political life*, Goetheanism could work everywhere . . . [author's italics]'.[9] If these words were taken seriously enough by some Europeans today, the way in which people live together on this continent—at least in some areas of life—could take on a form more appropriate to the times in which we live.

Appendix

Behind the Mask of Patriotism

During the First World War Rudolf Steiner used to quote a saying by Fichte: 'One *is* an Englishman, one *is* a Frenchman or an Italian, one can only *become* a German.' Unlike the peoples of southern, eastern and western Europe, the peoples of central Europe have continuously to concern themselves with difficult questions of identity. Germans especially have had no peace from such questions since the end of the eighteenth century.

The reasons for this lie partly in the being of the German folk spirit and its relationship to the German people: it is just because it is the task of the central Europeans to develop the powers of free initiative and the free individuality—from which is born the challenge to find the right connection between the world of the senses and the world of the spirit—that the German people have not been given their connection to their folk spirit as a birthright but have to seek it out actively. This folk spirit is, in contradistinction to other folk spirits, hardly to be experienced at all in the physical realm. It resides as a rule in the spiritual worlds and only seldom, as for example during the time of Goethe, does it work directly into the physical world.[1] At other times the Germans are—more than other peoples—exposed to influences from other spirits, which are often not in harmony with the aims of the central European folk spirit.

It is not in the least surprising then that the spiritual culture of central Europe is, in the absence of its 'guardian angel', continuously confronted by adversarial powers. The German folk spirit gives its people the possibility, which is at the same time a responsibility, to develop themselves as free human individualities. For although its impulses can only from time to time be felt directly on the earth, they can be perceived continuously in the spiritual world by anyone who *independently* seeks them out. Yet in the twentieth century such efforts were only made by a small number of people. The overwhelming majority of the Germans unconsciously expected—and still expect today—to receive a collective impulse from their folk spirit. Since this wish is one that, by its very nature, cannot be fulfilled, other spirits then enter the resultant vacuum. For in the soul of a people, just as in the soul of an individual person, a vacuum cannot last for long.

'The inner opposition to central Europe' is no easy theme to tackle. And yet what would be the result of leaving such a cardinal question untouched at the end of the twentieth century? In what follows we shall try to shed light on some aspects of this question and its history in this century. But first we must say something concerning the 'outer opposition'.

The Need for Opposition

Again and again various powers have placed obstacles in the way of a 'culture of spiritual independence', which can also be called a 'culture of the I Am', Rudolf Steiner described, for example, three historic phases during which the impulse in central Europe could only unfold itself in opposition to other forces.[2] Up until the time of Luther the Catholic Church ruled with absolute power in central Europe. When the Reformation made such surprisingly rapid progress in central Europe it was therefore held, in southern Europe, to be an especially dangerous challenge to Roman theocracy. Leaders of the Reformation such as Huss, Luther and others could, against this background, be counted among the pioneers of the central European 'self-determination'.

[margin handwriting: Roman Catholicism]

The second emancipation of central Europe, this time from French influence, came around the time of Lessing. Up until the eighteenth century central Europe had been dominated by French culture; the German literati wrote in French. Lessing, Herder, Goethe and their contemporaries were the first to write great literature in the German language. This took place at a time of mighty cultural renewal in central Europe. The German folk spirit was at that time fully active on the earth, and the Goethean world view went on to influence people right across the world—not just in central Europe.

Rudolf Steiner perceived a third opposition in the 'great discrepancy . . . between those who conduct experiments with matter and the like and seek thereby to prove the spiritual, and those who seek to raise impulses from the human soul life towards the spiritual'.[3] Anthroposophy belongs to the latter. Rudolf Steiner regarded its full unfolding in central Europe as a historical necessity of the twentieth century. But the opposition coming from the forces of what is a 'merely commercial element', this time from the Anglo-Saxon world, have striven to prevent this new emancipation of central Europe. Steiner has often described how certain groups in the West wish to keep the spiritual life of central Europe firmly under their control until far into the future. One can quite justifiably say, without being in any way clairvoyant, that the influence of western materialism has made the culture of central Europe (and in particular that of the reunited Germany) even more materialistic than that of the British, in which one can still find certain ideals that have arisen out of its folk characteristics. The materialism of the West thus represents a third force of opposition to the unfolding of the potential spiritual culture of central Europe since the Middle Ages.

*

Steiner described the dangers threatening the true culture of central Europe even more precisely when he spoke about certain grey and black occultists from both the East and the West and their battle for the Centre.[4] But nevertheless if one regards world development as a stage upon which the forces of freedom and necessity both play a part and in which quite divergent impulses are intertwined, one can understand these forces of opposition from a higher point of view. Rudolf Steiner described the three above-mentioned forces of opposition as a *necessity*[5] since, especially where a culture of freedom is to develop, there must also be the possibility given to fall into error. It belongs to the fate of the German people that they will be confronted with *forces of seduction* from all sides, for it is not only on account of its geographical position that Germany is exposed to the largest possible number of influences. The cause for this lies more in the existence of a certain 'vacuum culture' in central Europe, which was originally created for the development of the free human individuality.

Learning to Distinguish Between the Folk Spirit
and the Folk Demon

The specific talents of every people play an important role in the evolution of humanity. The different peoples are thus able to contribute something of real significance to the common growth and development of civilization. At certain times particular peoples play key roles in the unfolding of this historical drama. In accordance with its talents and task, each people should at the right historical moment take up its role in such a way that it thereby helps the *whole* of humanity in its further development.

The reality, however, often looks quite different. The different peoples often intervene at the wrong time and in an inappropriate manner in the whole drama, sometimes even taking on the role of another people and, in doing so, cause much strife and disturbance on the world stage. From time to time such disturbances then lead to wars.

Those nonetheless wishing to recognize the role of the folk spirits in this war-torn world have to answer a difficult question. How can one explain the at times tragic deviation of certain peoples from their roles and from the ideal harmony that should exist between them and other peoples? It was actually during the First World War that Steiner described the folk spirits as pupils gathered around a master teacher.[6]

Some of the great catastrophes of recent times must be put down to the influences of quite different beings. Especially since the last third of the nineteenth century, many beings of a luciferic and an ahrimanic nature have intervened in the life of the different peoples and have inspired the rise of nationalism, chauvinism and racism.[7] _While doing that they misuse, often in the cleverest way imaginable, just those talents that each people has been given for their own ends._ An interesting example here is the history of Great Britain from the last third of the nineteenth century up until the middle of this century.

The world of the eighteenth and nineteenth centuries was a treasure trove for the English, a place of unlimited natural resources and 'undiscovered' countries to be conquered and owned as one's private property. However, in the last third of the previous century there developed in England a quite different conviction. Now mere ownership and wealth were no longer the essentials. Everywhere people spoke of the 'glory and greatness' of the unified world Empire and of a holy mission to bring British culture and language to the 'uncivilized' parts of the globe. The idealistic striving of William Gladstone (the Liberal prime minister during 1868–74, 1880–85, 1886 and 1892–94) and some other Britons to pursue—in spite of everything—a humanitarian statecraft was an almost total failure. People such as Disraeli, Rosebery and Rhodes generated a national ecstasy through which a new form of imperialism—*neo-imperialism*—was able to take hold. But these personalities stood under the influence of certain occult circles, who had purposefully sought to misuse just those qualities that the British had been given in order to play their true role! Rudolf Steiner once described just this very phenomenon: 'These occult brotherhoods do not work out of any particular patriotism since their aim is to place the whole earth under the dominion of materialism. And since in accordance with the laws of the fifth post-Atlantean epoch certain elements of the British people are best suited to be bearers of the consciousness soul, those occult brotherhoods wish to bring it about that, through the use of grey magic, just these elements can be used to promote materialism.'[8] The fact that it was a fairly long time before the British finally gave up the ecstasy of neo-imperialism belongs to the tragedies of our age. Just like many other peoples today, they are faced with the task of learning to distinguish between the true folk spirit and other spirits of an ahrimanic and luciferic nature (the so-called folk demons).

When the Folk Spirit Leaves the Temple

When Rudolf Steiner spoke, in early 1914, of the 'malignant growth' and 'cultural cancer' of the materialistic culture of Europe[9] he had already perceived, as he later recalled, the threatening shadows of the First World War. The spirits of materialism and nationalism had long been busy all over Europe since the middle of the nineteenth century. War then raged for four years in Europe, leaving rubble, pain and confusion in its wake. The cultural cancer, a cold ahrimanic illness, spread so far that an overreaction in the form of a total war was now unavoidable. If one recognizes the true background to this tragedy, namely, the increased activity of the European folk demons since the 1840s, then the question of 'war guilt' is no longer of any relevance. For neither the West nor the East nor the Centre was in fact guilty.

When the war had finally ended, Rudolf Steiner began a movement for social renewal. The 'threefolding' of the social organism was intended to avert the possibility of future catastrophes through the healing of the economic and political realms, which would then aid the development of the free individuality. Such a healing was needed above all in central Europe, but the critical historical moment was not recognized.

After the threefold movement had more or less been rejected in Germany in 1921, Rudolf Steiner was still able for a while to hold public lectures there. But at the beginning of 1922 there was a sweeping change in the atmosphere in Germany. The rejection of the threefold ideal and its healing effects left a vacuum into which doubt and confusion flowed; they were good times for the spirits of collectivism. All this was by way of preparation for a much sharper attack on central Europe.

If only they had been awake enough to it, anthroposophists could have received significant indications of the coming danger in 1922, immediately after the rejection of the threefold idea as the only realistic option. In May, Rudolf Steiner was on a lecture tour across Germany. He held public lectures in large cities, including Munich, where anthroposophists had originally intended to build the Goetheanum. It was there that the heart of the anthroposophical movement was intended to beat; it was there that the Mystery Dramas had been written and performed. Yet already in 1921 nationalist, racist groupings such as the Thule Society and the National Socialist Party (newly founded as the NSDAP in February 1920) had become dangerously popular, and Hans Buchenbacher warned Steiner that he was number 8 or 9 'on the list of prominent personalities who were to be shot'. Steiner replied calmly 'yes, so it will be'.[10] Despite this, he came to Munich on 15 May 1922 where he gave a lecture at the Four Seasons Hotel, which the 'mother of National Socialism', the Thule-Society, used for its gatherings. At the end of the lecture, hired boxers and wrestlers and anthroposophical friends were only just able to save Rudolf Steiner from the planned attempt on his life. A short battle then broke out with the assailants, during which the policemen who were present did nothing. The following morning, two hours earlier than planned, Steiner had to leave Munich;[11] he never returned.

A week later, after further organized attacks against him in cities throughout Germany on his tour, especially in Elberfeld, Rudolf Steiner spoke stern words of exhortation and warning to the anthroposophists in Stuttgart:

Humanity needs to take up that which flows down from the spiritual heights into earthly life. It can be rejected. If it is rejected there then ceases for those people who have rejected it the possibility of human progress, of cultural progress, of human civilization, and the further development of humanity will have to be sought among *other peoples, and in other areas* . . . We can see today among ourselves how a huge battle has now begun over that which Anthroposophy wills to spread, a battle whose protagonists can only be overcome *if one tears away the masks from their faces at the right time* . . . I could mention many other sides from which one fights [against Anthroposophy] . . . But now there is beginning a battle for which the other one, which I have just characterized, was just a precursor. Such a battle is beginning now and one should not be under any illusions about the nature of this battle . . .[12]

By then it was already clear which powers were striving for power in central Europe. They were not just attacking by means of seduction any more. They wished to annihilate the true impulse of central Europe and knew exactly that they must silence Steiner as a high representative of this impulse. In part they did indeed attain their aim: Rudolf Steiner was unable to hold any more public lectures in Germany after May 1922; it had become too dangerous for him. From then until his death almost the only trips to Germany he made were to Stuttgart and they were kept out of the public eye. During that decisive period other spiritual powers were active in Germany, and the destruction of the Goetheanum through fire took place at this decisive time (on 31 December 1922). Certainly, ten months later, on 9 November 1923, the attempt by Hitler to make the Bavarian Government as a state independent of Berlin failed, the NSDAP was banned and Hitler himself was sentenced to five years in jail. But he was granted early release and on Rudolf Steiner's last birthday (27 February 1925) the NSDAP celebrated their refounding.

*

A new phase of the Sun Spirit's ever-increasing activity in the development of humanity was prepared for during the first decade of the twentieth century. In 1909 the first signs of the approach of the Sun Spirit in the etheric realm were apparent.[13] For Steiner it was a real and decisive question of historical development that people, especially the inhabitants of central Europe, should be adequately prepared for this event. It was for this reason that he spoke in several lectures after January 1910 of the reappearance of Christ in the etheric realm. This reappearance would be noticed by a few people during the 30s and then by more and more thereafter. He attempted to show his listeners how absolutely vital an increase in the 'I am'-consciousness of humanity was as a preparation for a conscious perceiving of the Sun Spirit in the etheric world.

Steiner also spoke about the opponents of the Sun Spirit at the same historic moment. Probably because he was aware of the tendency of people to emotional overreactions, he only very occasionally spoke of the Sun Demon, who at this time was also entering a wholly new field of activity. The significance of the impulses from this being for humanity in the twentieth century would be almost impossible to over-estimate (as is also the case for the Sun Being Himself). Already when Steiner spoke about the rhythm of 666 in connection with the being of the Sun Demon, his listeners would have been able to guess that it was above all the twentieth century that he had in mind.

The great difference between the activity of the Sun De-mon in the past and in the twentieth century was described in detail by Steiner in September 1924, when he held his last lectures.[14] The principle of the Sun Demon (named Sorath) works to begin with through beings of an ahrimanic and a luciferic nature. This happens for two reasons: firstly be-cause the time for the full revelation of his destructive power lies in the still distant future;[15] and secondly, because one should conceive the actual opponent of the Sun Spirit as a being who relates very differently to Lucifer and Ahriman. For while the Sun Being seeks to hold Lucifer and Ahriman in balance in order to show humanity the mid-way between these two powers of seduction, Sorath sends Lucifer and Ahriman to humanity so that their powers of *seduction* can prepare the way for his *destructive* onslaughts. For this reason then, the forces of Lucifer and Ahriman have been much more visible in the past than those of the Sun Demon. Only in the twentieth century is humanity for the first time partly exposed to Sorath without his luciferic or ahrimanic masks. For the first time many people experience the differ-ence between *the forces of seduction and the forces of destruction.* For while Ahriman strives to bring the earth to such a point of material rigidity that no human 'I' can dwell on it and Lucifer wishes to entice people to his own planet of light,[16] Sorath's aim is to annihilate the human 'I' and the earth. As the actual opponent of the Sun Spirit he seeks to destroy the human 'I am', bearer of the Sun-Impulse in the human being, and its place of development, the earth.

The new phase of Sorath's activity began quite clearly at the beginning of the century. At the time of the First World War people possessed by the Sun Demon began to draw attention to themselves, they began to set the scene: the lust for destruction with which the battles of the Western Front were fought (as seen, for example, in the policy of blood-shedding for the sake of attrition in the battle of Verdun and the massive use of poison gas as a weapon of war) was a symptom of this. Bolshevism, which Steiner described as a concentrated seed form of the Sorathic phenomenon, was already more than a symptom.[17] Yet the year in which Sorath, according to Rudolf Steiner, would actually make his appearance was 1933. In this decisive year for the appearance of Christ in the etheric realm, Sorath would, according to Steiner, 'arise from the abyss'.[18]

Hitler Jan. 1933

The People Without an Immune System

As the year 1933 approached, the alluring powers of the folk demons were on the march throughout Europe. Behind their activities one could everywhere observe how the powers of the Sun Demon here and there made an inroad. The Fascist regime of Mussolini in Italy and the other nationalist and Fascist movements in countries such as Spain, France and England did not any more *just* reckon on the naivety of their followers. Increasingly, one could see how those who had been called 'Sorath people' by Steiner came forward with 'furious gestures and a lust for destruction in their emotions'.[19]

In this situation the German people were an exception. Unlike the other peoples of Europe they did not possess a 'collective guardian angel' on the earth, which would have afforded them some protection against the destructive impulses coming from Sorath. In contrast to the time of Fichte, the German folk spirit is in the spiritual worlds during this century. He must be searched for there and can, as a rule, 'only be found with the help of spiritual science'.[20] It was in just this situation that the special task of the Germans was made even harder: they were called upon to develop their 'I am' forces particularly strongly. Sorath strives particularly strongly against this: he wishes to destroy the Christ-impulse in human beings, and this is closely associated with the development of the 'I am'.

Against this background one can understand the particular intensity with which the Sorathic influence came up in Germany.[21] At that time these powers were seeking to gain a real foothold over all in Europe, and yet nowhere were they able to gain such a strong hold as in Hitler's Germany in which they seized the mood of the people and even a part of the 'folk emotion' itself. It was, for example, Mussolini's march on Rome in 1922 that marked the violence of Fascism. Yet even in this case the Sorathic forces were unable to overcome the forces of immunity due to the presence of the folk spirit within that people. Despite its tempestuous rise, Italian Fascism was always characterized by a certain moderation and a strong adherence to tradition. In Germany, by contrast, the National Socialists managed to take the bearers of culture and tradition (academics, churchmen and the middle classes) so far down the road with them that they silently acquiesced and often even actively helped in the acts of persecution and annihilation against political opponents, the sick, invalids, 'non-Aryans' and—finally—against the German people itself.

In Germany the absence of its collective guardian angel produces among the people an unconscious atmosphere of perpetual anxiety. In contrast to the French or the English, in whom a certain self-confidence as a people can overcome collective anxiety, even in the most difficult of moments, the Germans can *as a group* easily lose their balance in such

situations. In this sense, then, 1933 provided the possibility
for an epidemic to spread across Germany that was worse
than the ahrimanic cultural cancer: the German people
were now to become the organism for the Sorathic epidemic, which can be clearly compared to the AIDS epidemic. For here was a people without a 'normal immune
system'. And its meagre powers of resistance could be
overcome with a few well-placed blows. One need only
think how the wave of fear and hysteria after the burning
of the Reichstag in 1933 (again on 27 February!) made
possible the passing of the 'Emergency Decree for the Protection of State and People' on the following day. In this
decree the basic rights of the Weimar constitution were
suspended, and the death penalty was introduced for a
variety of 'punishable deeds'. After a long phase of preparation the Germans were now gripped by the epidemic of
the Sun Demon.

If one attempts today to distance oneself from the
behaviour of the German population at that time by
saying that the people reacted irrationally, and that even
the anthroposophists had not recognized the full import
of the danger, then one is not just deceiving oneself in
respect to the past but also in regard to the present. For the
propaganda of the National Socialists was in itself most
definitely rationally and logically constructed! After the
Reichstag fire, for example, the famous constitutional lawyer Carl Schmidt published a lucid, scientifically grounded
piece arguing for the necessity of the emergency decree.
One recalls how convincing the National Socialist world
view was for a philosopher like Heidegger. Rational
thinking could then, as today, only be of help to those
who were, as individualities, sufficiently developed to
recognize the underlying spiritual realities, namely, *the
destructive will* that lies behind that specific logic. A sense
for *spiritual realities* was necessary in order to see through
the brilliant deceptions. Unfortunately, though, one cannot

automatically achieve this sense by reading the work of Rudolf Steiner! Those few who had formed such a power of perception were the first to be dealt with. As long as only a handful of Germans had an individual contact with the folk spirit, the German people *as a group* did not possess an organ for the spiritual. The people *as a whole* were unable to recognize the spiritual realities behind the 'patriotic logic' of the adversary.

*

During the last phase of the war the Sun Demon, the greatest opponent of central Europe, finally threw off his ahrimanic-luciferic mask. This happened when Hitler, in March 1945, 'in complete calmness and clarity',[22] ordered the 'Final Solution' to be implemented against the German people. Now every thinking person knew: the greatest forces of opposition to central Europe come neither from the East nor from the West but from within! Worse than the physical destruction was the spiritual-soul desert which National Socialism had left behind it in the former cultural centre of central Europe.

During the years after 1945 the Germans were protected from outside against a collective epidemic and its attendant dangers. The political particularities of the post-war years once again gave individuals certain opportunities for *individual* development. The division of Germany and the East-West conflict more or less killed off any further possibilities of a collective epidemic. However, parallel to the fall of the Berlin Wall (on 9 November 1989, exactly 66 years after the Munich *putsch*) the Sorathic force of destruction once again appeared across Europe. It was, of course, present in one way or another during the Cold War: in Europe predominantly through the ever-present threat of destruction posed by atomic weapons, while in Russia and Asia regimes of terror (such as that in Cambodia) sent millions to their deaths. Today it is showing itself in the senseless physical, soul and spiritual destruction of countries like Bosnia-Hercegovina, Afghanistan, Rwanda, and Chechenia, in which forces of pure destruction are again lurking behind the mask of patriotism. Sometimes the people involved even admit this themselves!

*

The year 1998 stands immediately in front of us, and once again the anti-spirit of collectivism and with it the danger of losing inner balance begins to make itself present in Germany. In the days and weeks after the murders in Solingen on 30 May 1993 (the birthplace of Adolf Eichmann, who is still revered as an idol by the Right) one could clearly perceive with what disturbing ease certain forces used the general climate of fear and doubt. That is not to say that a collective Sorathic epidemic is about to spread in the same way as it did in the 30s. The outer conditions are altogether different! However, are the central Europeans now less naive? Are they harder to manipulate? Are they in a better position to recognize the spiritual realities behind the mask of patriotism? The answers to these questions will not be long in coming.

Notes

GA = *Gesamtausgabe*: the collected edition of Rudolf Steiner's works in the original German (published by Rudolf Steiner Verlag, Dornach, Switzerland).

Introduction

1. See especially those lectures given between 1914 and 1924.
2. An example of this is the destruction of Warsaw in August and September 1944 by troops of the SS. About 150,000 people were murdered in an action that took place under an SS command that consisted of many different European nationals. As Michael Foedrowitz wrote in the German weekly *Die Zeit* (29 July 1994), 'It was as if people were enacting scenes straight from Dante's inferno. Drunken Ukrainians danced in shop window displays and raped women and girls. Furniture, cutlery and people were thrown out of windows. In a frenzy of blood and alcohol everything was killed, beaten, shot, crushed under foot . . . German army sappers let gas into the sewers and set light to it. Whole roads collapsed . . . One of the sappers whose unit had been joined by a troop of flame-throwers recalled that: "captured insurgents and civilians were mercilessly burnt alive". This was called "bandit burnings". A few fire officers suffered severe shocks. They were taken away from the front and "hidden away in the Reich".' See also Chapter 6 on 'Solidarity'.
3. Wilhelm Muehlon, *Tagebuch der Kriegsjahre* (Diary of the war years), edited by Jens Heisterkamp, Dornach 1992, p. xxviii (Introduction).

Chapter 1

1. During his studies as a Rhodes Scholar he would have had

the best opportunity to get to know the Anglo-Saxon origins of American values in England. (See also Chapter 2.)

2. Oxford, as the oldest university in the English-speaking world, is indeed the archetype of the American university system. At least five other close co-workers of the original Clinton administration were graduates from Oxford. Some studied there as Rhodes Scholars (such as CIA chief R. James Woolsey, who is also a Yale graduate; or Labor Secretary Robert Reich, who studied in Oxford together with Clinton from 1968 to 1970).

3. Lecture of 22 October 1909 (GA 58), *Metamorphosis of the Soul*, Vol. 1, Rudolf Steiner Press, London 1983.

4. Lecture of 21 August 1917 (GA 176), *The Karma of Materialism*, Rudolf Steiner Press, London 1985.

5. Skull and Bones (the emblem of the Skull and Bones is one of the original symbols of Freemasonry) is often spoken of and written about too flippantly. Many world-conspiracy theorists and sundry anti-Anglo-Americans try in this way to confirm their paranoid feelings of fear and hatred. It is also generally recognized that the Nazis—as well as their successors—are extreme examples of what such an obsessively driven occupation with such themes can produce. It is nonetheless important for our present study to make ourselves acquainted with some of the facts relating to this 'senior society'.

6. Rudy Abramson, *Spanning the Century, The Life of W.A. Harriman*, New York 1992, p. 103f.

7. W. Isaacson and E. Thomas, *The Wise Men—Six Friends and the World They Made*, New York 1986, p. 82.

8. The famous orator Demosthenes (384–322 BC) was one of the most influential opponents of Philip of Macedonia and his son Alexander the Great. Immediately after Alexander's death (323 BC) he initiated another coup in Athens, the failure of which forced him to flee. He then committed suicide in order to avoid being executed.

9. Pamela (née Digby 1920) Churchill-Hayward-Harriman and Averell Harriman were already in 1941 more than well-acquainted with one another. At the time she was married to

Churchill's son Randolf. Her husband was out on active service and she was living with the prime minister at 10 Downing Street. During the war Averell Harriman was in close contact with and often stayed with Churchill, even living for a time in London. It was not until 1971, a few months after they had both lost their spouses, that the Harrimans met and decided to marry (he was 81 and she was 51). See also: Christopher Ogden, *Life of the Party, The Biography of Pamela Digby Churchill Hayward Harriman*, London 1994.

10. *Washington Post*, 6 November 1992.
11. Lecture of 4 December 1920 (GA 202), not translated.
12. Some people hold the view that even the very existence of the secret societies of the West referred to by Steiner is a closely guarded secret. To maintain such a level of secrecy in today's world is, however, all but impossible (as was already the case at the beginning of this century). Today one can at most attempt to ignore questions concerning them (as was done by White House spokespersons during the Bush presidency). But Steiner had in mind something else when he spoke about the secrecy of such orders: 'This spiritual community keeps itself very secret, not so much in order to serve its continued existence, *but in accordance with its inner impulses*' (lecture of 21 February 1920, GA 196, not translated). It is in no way asserted here that 'Skull and Bones' is *the* secret society of the West. This influential brotherhood is merely one of a number of groups that are under the influence of certain spiritual beings. It is, however, one of the most effective *external* instruments of a spiritual stream that makes use of groups and channels of the most varied sort. One must also be clear that the number of people in this stream who are acting in full consciousness is very small. (See R. Steiner's lecture of 20 January 1917, GA 174, *The Karma of Untruthfulness*, Vol. 2, Rudolf Steiner Press, London 1922, in which he says: 'It is always only a small number of people who are entrusted with these things, for such societies are as a rule organized so that the ceremonial magic will work specially on those who least suspect it.')
13. See Note 3.

Chapter 2

1. See George Adams, 'Rudolf Steiner in England', in *A Man Before Others*. *Rudolf Steiner Remembered*, Rudolf Steiner Press, London 1993.
2. See the nine lectures given in Manchester College, Oxford, 12–25 August 1922 (GA 305), *The Spiritual Ground of Education*, Garber, New York 1989.
3. Cecil Rhodes (1853–1902). On account of ill health he set forth from England to South Africa already in 1871. Between 1873 and 1881 he studied at Oxford. His work on the South African diamond fields forced him continuously to take long breaks from his studies. In 1884 he became the finance minister to the Cape Colony; from 1888 he controlled the whole diamond production of the country (which at that time corresponded to 93% of the global diamond production); in 1890 he became prime minister. At the same time he received a mandate as a member of the British Parliament.
4. W.T. Stead, *The Last Will and Testament of Cecil John Rhodes*, London 1902, p. 74–76.
5. See D. Leon, *John Ruskin, the Great Victorian*, London 1949.
6. See Note 4.
7. See, for example, the lecture of 17 December 1916 (GA 173), *The Karma of Untruthfulness*, Vol. 1, Rudolf Steiner Press, London 1988.
8. John Marlow, *Cecil Rhodes. The Anatomy of Empire*, London 1972, p. 211.
9. Ignatius Loyola, the founder of the Society of Jesus (1491–1556).
10. See J. Marlow, p. 64.
11. Professor Carroll Quigley (1910–77). Taught at the Foreign Service School of Georgetown University as well as at the famous universities of Harvard and Princeton.
12. H.V. Hodson, 'The Round Table 1910–1981', from *The Round Table*, October 1981. (The periodical still exists to this day.)
13. See Rudolf Steiner's lecture from 21 August 1924 (GA 240) in Torquay, *Karmic Relationships*, Vol. VIII, Rudolf Steiner Press, London 1975, p. 38.

14. Quigley's second book, *The Evolution of Civilizations, An Introduction to Historical Analysis,* was also written in Oxford. In the Foreword to the first edition (1961) he expressly thanked Professor H.L. Rowse of All Souls College for his help. According to Quigley this college has been the most strongly influenced by the Rhodes-Milner group.
15. See C.F. Allen, *The Comeback Kid. The Life and Career of Bill Clinton,* New York 1992.
16. Robert E. Levin, *Bill Clinton—The Inside Story,* New York 1992, p. 49.
17. Quoted from Ivor Benson, 'Window on the World', from the periodical *The Covenant Message,* June 1977.
18. According to a statement of Clinton's. See C.F. Allen. Senator James William Fulbright, who died on 9 February 1995 at the age of 89, was the founder of an internationally renowned student exchange programme named after himself, which was in reality an expansion and continuation of the Rhodes Scholarship. Next to Carroll Quigley he played the most important role in the education of Bill Clinton, something that Clinton fully acknowledged after his death: 'Without him I would not be where I am today,' he said.
19. Until the death of Rhodes the society was concerned in the first instance with the planning of its activities. The first phase of its actual development began in 1902 with Milner's practical fulfilment of these plans and ended in 1925 with his death. These historical dates and the fact that Rhodes House was built between 1925 and 1928 bear an uncanny similarity to the dates of the development of the anthroposophical movement.
20. See Chapter 1.
21. According to a recent report from UNESCO.

Chapter 3

1. *International Herald Tribune,* 1 November 1993, p. 7.
2. See GA 196, lecture of 9 January 1920, not translated.
3. Huntington, on his own admission, has taken the concept

'civilization' from the famous historian Arnold J. Toynbee (1889–1975), who divides up the world into 21 different civilizations and societies. Toynbee was a prominent member of the Rhodes-Milner group. ('The Round Table', see Chapter 2.)

4. Arthur M. Schlesinger, Jr, *A Thousand Days*, London 1965, p. 115. Unlike the *Foreign Affairs* journal which is the official periodical of the Council on Foreign Relations, *The New York Times* is not of course an official mouthpiece for the Establishment.

5. The Council on Foreign Relations was founded in 1921 by members and supporters of the Round Table movement and was moulded on the British Royal Institute of International Affairs.

6. For Averell Harriman see Chapter 1 of this book.

7. See Walter Isaacson and Evan Thomas, *The Wise Men—Six Friends and the World They Made*, New York 1986, pp. 347–438.

8. See Chapter 1 for more on these brotherhoods.

9. *The Wise Men*, pp. 407–08. Isaacson and Thomas are in no way critics of the Establishment, far more are they to be counted as insiders and respecters of the Wise Men. Isaacson is a Rhodes Scholar and works (since January 1996) as Managing Editor of *Time* magazine, and Thomas is a Harvard graduate and is an editor at *Newsweek*.

10. Professor Samuel Philip Huntington studied at the elite universities of Harvard and Yale and has for many years now been the Director of the Institute for Strategic Studies at Harvard University. He was also for a while a Fellow of All Souls College in Oxford (for the connection between All Souls and the Rhodes-Milner group see p. 25) and has regularly led working groups in the Council on Foreign Relations.

11. For an analysis of this map see the article by Terry M. Boardman in *Das Goetheanum*, No. 33/34 of 14 August 1994.

12. See Note 2.

13. Rudolf Steiner, lecture of 4 April 1916 (GA 167), not translated.

Chapter 4

1. On 3 January 1994 *The New York Times* reported how the so-

called 'Partnership for Peace' had finally been adopted as the official strategy of the USA. Strobe Talbott, a close friend of Bill Clinton, with whom he had lived as a 'Rhodes Scholar' in Oxford, wrote a memorandum on 17 October 1993. Talbott, then roving 'ambassador at large' in eastern Europe, and today (the end of 1994) Warren Christopher's deputy, was able to force through his plan against the opinion of the secretary of state which was that NATO should open to the East without delay or reservation.
2. See Chapter 6 on Masaryk for a contemplation on such ideas.

Chapter 5

1. Wilhelm Muehlon, *Ein Fremder im eigenen Land, Erinnerungen und Tagebuchaufzeichnungen* 1908–1914 (edited by Wolfgang Benz), Bremen 1989, p. 98f.
2. See Polzer-Hoditz, *Das Testament Peters des Großen*, Dornach 1989.
3. See Note 1.
4. Charles Krauthammer, 'The UN Obsession', *Time* magazine, 9 May 1994.
5. *Süddeutsche Zeitung*, 12 April 1994.
6. Jim Hoagland, 'On Russia, at Least, Clinton's Grasp has been Firm', *Washington Post*, 1 June 1994.

Chapter 6

1. Karel Capek, *Gespräche mit T.G. Masaryk*, Munich 1969.
2. Ibid., p. 71.
3. From the lecture of 18 September 1924 (GA 346). Not published in English.
4. T.G. Masaryk, *Die Weltrevolution. Erinnerungen und Betrachtungen 1914–18*, Berlin 1927, pp. 371–72.
5. Ibid., pp. 375 and 350–51.
6. Ibid., p. 371.
7. See Thomas Meyer, *Ludwig Polzer-Hoditz, Ein Europäer*, Basel 1995.

8. See R. Steiner, lecture from 11 April 1919 (GA 190), not translated; and 25 December 1920 (GA 202), *The Search for the New Isis*, Mercury Press, New York 1983

9. E. Kohak, 'Masaryk und die Monarchie', in: Josef Novak (editor), *On Masaryk*. Texts in English and German, Amsterdam 1988.

10. *Weltrevolution*, pp. 284–85.

11. Ibid., p. 462.

12. The population comprised 46% Czechs, 13% Slovaks, 28% Germans, 8% Magyars (or Hungarians), 3% Jews, 3% Ukrainians and other smaller population groups.

13. Lecture of 22 August 1920 (GA 199), in *Spiritual Science as a Foundation for Social Forms*, Anthroposophic Press, New York 1986.

14. Lecture of 21 August 1920 (GA 199), as above.

15. Gerald B. Helman and Steven R. Ratner, 'Saving Failed States', *Foreign Policy*, No. 89, Winter 1992–93.

16. It could be argued that nationalism and imperialism existed earlier. But when these phenomena are analysed more exactly, one is justified in maintaining that their present form has changed, and that in this form they are being fed by forces which, historically, are to be designated as new.

17. Lecture of 22 September 1924 (see Note 3).

18. See Note 1, p.317.

19. This is not in any way to question the value of democratic principles. Whether, however, simple majority decisions alone can lead to justice in the economic life is certainly highly questionable.

Chapter 7

1. *Basler Zeitung*, 2 August 1994.

2. W. Isaacson and E. Thomas, *The Wise Men—Six Friends and the World They Made*, New York 1986, p. 223.

3. W. Averell Harriman and Elie Abel, *Special Envoy to Churchill and Stalin 1941–1946*, New York 1975, p. 289f.

4. William Larsh, 'W. Averell Harriman and the Polish Question, December 1943–August 1944', *East European Politics and*

Societies, Vol. 7, No. 3, Fall 1993, p. 513f.

5. Ibid., p. 517.
6. Ibid., pp. 526–27.
7. *The Wise Men*, p. 223.
8. Larsh, p. 533.
9. Author's italics. Ibid., p. 539. See also p. 552.
10. Ibid., p. 542.
11. Ibid., p. 547f.
12. Ibid., p. 549.
13. See Stefan Lubienski, 'Die Polnische Volksseele', *Blätter für Anthroposophie*, 11 Jahrgang (1959), p. 287.
14. From an answer to a question after a lecture in Stuttgart, 2 January 1921 (GA 338), not translated.
15. See R.E. Levin, *Bill Clinton, the Inside Story*, New York 1992, p. 35f.
16. See C.F. Allen and Jonathan Portis, *Bill Clinton, A Biography*.
17. R.E. Levin, p. 39.
18. For the relationship between Quigley and Clinton see Chapter 2.
19. R.E. Levin, p. 43f.
20. See D.A. Yallop, *In God's Name*, New York 1984. Since the beginning of the 1980s many books and articles have appeared on this subject. Since the election of Silvio Berlusconi, 'former' lodge member of P2, to the Italian premiership, such researches have notably increased. Although most of them ought to be considered as cheap scandal-mongering, they sometimes uncover significant facts which can be of use in understanding this particular 'landscape'.
21. Lecture given in Dornach, 3 July 1920 (GA 198), not translated.
22. See, for example, the excellent description in Renate Riemeck's book *Moscow und der Vatican*, Basel 1978.
23. Tadeusz Mazowiecki, *Partei nehmen für die Hoffnung*, Freiburg 1990, p. 153.
24. Ibid., p. 176.
25. Carl Bernstein, 'The Holy Alliance', *Time International*, 24 February 1992.
26. Ibid., p. 16.
27. Ibid., p. 14.

28. Zbigniew Brzezinski worked initially with the Democrat President Carter. But in Washington ideological differences are of no importance when it comes to the *real* questions of what is in 'America's national interest'. See Chapter 1 for more on this.
29. Bernstein, p. 19.
30. Ibid., p. 17.
31. Ibid.
32. Ibid., p. 18.
33. Quoted from W. Bartoszewski, 'Kulturelle Vielfalt Versus Kulturelle Einheit Europas?' *TAZ*, Berlin, 2 April 1988 (author's italics).
34. See, for example, the article by Bartoszewski, which appeared before the Velvet Revolution.
35. Zbigniew Brzezinski, 'The Untimely Exclusion of Germany and Russia from a Friendly Fete', *International Herald Tribune*, 2 May 1994 (author's italics). This piece appeared as part of a special group of articles that were published to mark the anniversary of D-Day and concerned themselves with the future of European-American relations.
36. George Kolankiewicz, 'The Eastern Enlargement of the EU', *International Affairs*, Vol. 70, No. 3, July 1994.
37. See the leading article by Josef Joffe in the *Süddeutsche Zeitung* of 26 August 1993.
38. See *Time International*, 5 September 1994, p. 32.

Chapter 8

1. The words of Michael Sturmer, director of a research institute for international politics, in *Neue Zürcher Zeitung*, 24 September 1994.
2. For the complete quotation, see the previous chapter.
3. Stuart E. Eizenstat, 'The United States Backs the Process of European Integration', *International Herald Tribune*, 19 August 1994 (author's italics).
4. Rudolf Steiner, lecture of 18 October 1918 (GA 185), *From Symptom to Reality in Modern History*, Rudolf Steiner Press, London 1976.

NOTES

143

5. Quoted from Zbigniew Brzezinski, 'The Ripening Test', in *Die Zeit*, 8 July 1994.
6. *Proposals for European Policy*, Europe Document of the CDU/CSU party in the German Bundestag, 1 September 1994, pp. 8 and 10.
7. See Note 4. Lecture from 1 November 1918.
8. Ibid.
9. Ibid.

Appendix

1. See the lecture by Rudolf Steiner of 16 March 1915 in Berlin (GA 157), *The Destinies of Individuals and Nations*, Rudolf Steiner Press, London 1987.
2. Lecture of 15 January 1917 in Dornach (GA 174), *The Karma of Untruthfulness*, Vol. II, Rudolf Steiner Press, Sussex 1992.
3. Ibid.
4. See, for example, the lecture of 25 November 1917 (GA 178) or the lecture cycle, *The Occult Movement in the Nineteenth Century* (GA 254), Rudolf Steiner Press, London 1973.
5. See Note 2.
6. See the lecture of 13 September 1914, held in Munich (GA 174a), not translated.
7. See *Rudolf Steiner über den Nationalismus*, selected and edited by Karl Heyer, Perseus Verlag, Basel 1993.
8. See Note 2.
9. Lecture in Vienna on 14 April 1914 (GA 153), *The Inner Nature of Man and the Life Between Death and Rebirth*, Rudolf Steiner Press, Bristol 1994.
10. H. Büchenbacher, 'Begegnungen mit Rudolf Steiner 1920–1924', *Mitteilungen aus der Anthroposophischen Arbeit in Deutschland*, Michaelmas 1978.
11. Ibid.
12. 'Der Verfall des menschlichen Intellekts und das Sichwehren des Menschen gegen die Spiritualität' ('The fall of the human intellect and the rejection of spirituality'), lecture of 23 May 1922, held in Stuttgart. Published by Marie Steiner during World War II, Dornach 1942 (not translated).

13. See Steiner's lecture of 6 February 1917 (GA 175), *Cosmic and Human Metamorphosis*, Anthroposophical Publishing Company, London 1926.
14. *Apokalypse und Priesterwirken*, lecture cycle from 5 to 22 September 1924. The lectures were held for priests of the Christian Community and for members of the *Vorstand* of the Anthroposophical Society. They have now been published in German as a part of Rudolf Steiner's collected works (GA 346).
15. See the lecture of 29 June 1908 (GA 104), *The Apocalypse of St John*, Rudolf Steiner Press, London 1985.
16. See Rudolf Steiner's lecture of 17 September 1916 in Dornach (GA 171), *Inner Impulses of Evolution*, Anthroposophic Press, New York 1984.
17. See Note 14, lecture of 12 September 1924.
18. See Note 14, lecture of 20 September 1924. It is an interesting fact that already in his first lecture on the appearance of Christ in the etheric world (12 January 1910) Steiner spoke of the dangers associated with the year 1933 and of an endless 'confusion of soul'. He also said: 'In 1933 there will be many schools of black magic in which will be falsely proclaimed the physical reappearance of Christ.' (*Rudolf Steiner über die Wiederkunft Christi*, edited by Harold Giersch, Dornach 1991, p. 107f.)
19. See Note 17.
20. See Note 1.
21. See 'Der Kampf gegen das Ich', Chapter 2 in Karl Heyer's *Wesen und Wollen des Nationalsozialismus*, Basel 1991.
22. According to the General Chief of Staff Franz Halder, in W. Hofer (ed.) *Der Nationalsozialismus*, p. 264.

Index of Names

Stalin, J., 11, 12, 48, 79, 80, 81,
    82
Stead, W.T., 20, 23, 25
Steiner, R., 1f., 8, 15f., 21, 35,
    43, 67f., 72f., 74f., 86,
    89f., 105f., 116f., 119f.
Stewart Mill, J., 73
Stimson, H.C.L., 39

Taft, W.H., 9
Thatcher, M., 35
Thibaud, P., 91
Thomas, E., 41

Trentowski, 86
Truman, H.S., 12, 38, 39
Tudjman, 113

Walesa, L., 79, 94, 95
Walters, V., 95
Wilson, W., 96
Wilson, Woodrow, 12
Winant, J.G., 82
Wojtyla, K., see John Paul II

Yeltsin, B., 51

Index of Places